THE FATHER
AND HIS FAMILY

The Father and his Family

A Guidebook for Aspiring, New, and Experienced Fathers

by Michael Moynihan

Scepter

Published by Scepter Publishers, Inc.
info@scepterpublishers.org
www.scepterpublishers.org
800-322-8773
New York

Text and cover design by Christina Aquilina

ISBN pb 978-1-59417-283-0
ebook 978-1-59417-284-7

Library of Congress Cataloging-in-Publication Data

Names: Moynihan, Michael (Michael Steven), 1969– author.
Title: The father and his family : a guidebook for aspiring, young, and old fathers / Michael Moynihan.
Description: New York : Scepter Pub, 2017.
Identifiers: LCCN 2017013784 (print) |
LCCN 2017022461 (ebook) | ISBN
9781594172847 (ebook) | ISBN 9781594172830 (pbk.)
Subjects: LCSH: Fathers—Religious life. | Fatherhood—Religious aspects—Christianity. | Catholic Church—Doctrines.
Classification: LCC BV4529.17 (ebook) |
LCC BV4529.17 .M69 2017 (print) | DDC
248.8/421—dc23
LC record available at https://lccn.loc.gov/2017013784

Printed in the United States of America.

Contents

ACKNOWLEDGMENTS

I would like to thank my wonderful wife Angela and my children, Michael, Thomas, Theresa, Joseph, Stephen, Elizabeth, John Paul, Lucy, Margaret, Patrick, and little Luke, all of whom were supportive in their own ways. This book would never have come about without them. Special thanks go to Alvaro deVicente for his sage advice and assistance, as well as Russell Shaw, Pat Fagan, Fr. Diego Daza, and Regis Flaherty for their editing help and input. I am very grateful to be working with Meredith Koopman and all those at Scepter who helped bring this project to fruition. I would also like to thank the countless fathers whom I have known and worked with through the Heights School community and elsewhere. And, of course, out of all these fathers, I owe the greatest debt of gratitude to my own father, Charles Moynihan, as well as my mother, Nancy Moynihan.

INTRODUCTION

The job of being a father is not an easy one. Fathers are expected to be providers and protectors, caring for their families and others. A typical father faces demands both at work and at home. After a long day at work, he returns home to the demands of family life, as well as its many joys. Tired though he is, family life requires additional energy, leadership, and understanding.

But as parents say nighttime prayers with their children and then, shortly afterwards, see them peacefully sleeping in their beds, they smile at each other, thinking over the day and knowing that all the sacrifices are worth it. Finally husband and wife enjoy some time conversing together and look forward to some well-deserved rest. Although, on some nights their sleep may be interrupted as they attend to the needs of their children, especially the younger ones.

So when all is well, being a parent is exhausting but very joyful and blessed. Seeing one's children grow and experiencing the warmth and love of one's family are certainly great treasures. But everything does not always go smoothly. Good men struggle with difficulties at work and with challenges at home. And those who are a bit older know that such struggles are often the norm rather than the exception. Most families have their own crosses, some hidden and some not, some brief in duration and others more ongoing. Financial difficulties may be a source of worry and even tension. It is not uncommon for one or more children in a family to go through difficult stages, whether it is the "terrible twos" or more serious difficulties during the teenage years. And from time to time in history there have been periods of strife—wars, economic depressions, or outbreaks of serious diseases—all of which have impacted families and have required great leadership and sacrifice from parents.

A typical father's life, as a whole, is one of great joy mixed with suffering. If a young man at the happy occasion of falling in love and beginning his married life could see before him all the hardships that the future holds he would probably be crushed under the weight of what lies ahead. But if he could also see the great joys and some of the fruit of his sacrificial fatherly love he would, hopefully, generously embrace all the hardships in spite of their weight. In reality, none of us have such clear vision into the future. We embark on a path, a vocation, with an unknown future before us. We walk and, at times, stumble forward. Those with faith know that we all live very much in the loving arms of our Father in heaven, and that in the end all things truly do work for the good for those who love him (ref. Rom 8:28).

I have been privileged to live through some of the adventure of fatherhood and to work with many families as an educator at The Heights School, a private, all-boys school in Potomac, Maryland. My wife Angela and I were married in 1995 and, after not being able to have children for the first few years of our marriage (we had our first child shortly after a few providential occurrences that followed Angela's brief meeting with St. Teresa of Calcutta), we recently welcomed our eleventh child on August 1, 2016. We have seven boys and four girls. The youngest was due around the time that our eldest, Michael, was to be leaving for college. We joked that we would name the baby Michael so that as one Michael was leaving another would take his place. Common sense prevailed, however, and we named the baby Luke.

It has certainly not always been easy being the father of a large family. Like any family, we have had our share of joys and difficulties. Overall I am incredibly thankful and know that I owe a great debt of gratitude to many other fathers, men I work with or have gotten to know through the Heights community. The Heights is a distinctive school with a group of parents who are committed to its mission to help form the saints and leaders our world needs, men who will go out into the world and transform society from within, men who will be strong fathers, skilled professionals, and good friends. The commitment to such a lofty mission goes hand in hand with knowing that boys, and indeed all of us, are very much works in progress, that we all will make mistakes and need to continually make adjustments and begin again. As the Head of the Upper School, I work with many families. Some are thriving and raising happy children despite the challenges present in our culture. Many are going through difficulties, some quite serious. And none are perfect.

In times past it was common for fathers to have a support network in some ways similar to the Heights community. Families tended to live in the same village for multiple generations. Life was simpler, centered in a community where people worked, worshipped, socialized, and lived in close proximity. Fathers benefited from wisdom and practical advice passed along in a natural way through the lived experiences of the community. I do not want to imply that the agrarian lifestyle of a typical nineteenth century European village was idyllic. And there are definite advantages people living today enjoy, including access to cultural riches that would astonish our ancestors. But the perennial voice of wisdom and perspective that was naturally passed along from one generation to another in times past is lacking today. Fathers often feel alone and overwhelmed, without an adequate support group. It can help to hear how other fathers have dealt with particular challenges. I know that I have benefited greatly by being able to bounce thoughts and ideas off so many experienced fathers at the Heights over the years.

In what follows I hope to pass on perspective that fathers can use, a second voice for generating ideas on how to deal with the challenges all fathers face today. This book is written as a handbook. Each chapter addresses different aspects of fatherhood. The book can be read from cover to cover or out of order. It follows a narrative approach at times, with examples from my own family and other families. Behind the advice and perspective is over twenty years of experience as an educator in a unique school, my own attempts to live out the vocation of fatherhood in my family, and a fair amount of reflection and study.

My experience in education has led me to believe that one of the most significant human challenges we face today is the need to integrate knowledge. Today people tend toward criticism more than synthesis, toward reducing things to component parts rather than trying to consider wholes, toward comfortably looking from different perspectives without struggling to reconcile and unify knowledge, and toward trying to determine how things work without adequate concern for what things are, with natures and essences.

It is particularly important to try to understand the nature of a thing so as to be able to better understand its proper functioning, what it exists for. Rather than rely on just one academic discipline, the best thinking comes when someone is open to the full scope of human reason. My approach is philosophical in the classical sense. I believe what is missing most from contemporary discourse is not any one particular approach or angle, but rather an eye open to examining the whole, open to consideration of "being." The classical name for the study of what exists, the study of being, is metaphysics. Today the science of metaphysics is little known or understood. In this book I attempt to present authentic fatherhood from a perspective open to using the full scope of human reason, which entails being open to philosophical and metaphysical considerations.[1]

---

1. Pope Benedict eloquently called for the restoration of the full scope of human reason in his "Regensburg Address," among other places. Benedict notes that the ultimate casualty of scientism (the belief that the methods of the empirical sciences are the only valid means to arrive at true statements) is the human person, who becomes "dehumanized" when the scope of his reason is reduced. His call to move beyond modern reductionism is echoed in Pope Francis's encyclical *Laudato Si*, where a call for us to respect nature is presented also as an invitation to respect the natural order that we discern in the world as a given, rather than seeking to dominate it and remake it through the imprudent use of technology. Ecology of nature should lead to a healthy human ecology, one that supports human reason open to seeing the world as created by God.

My experience over the years has reinforced my belief in a natural order that we humans did not make, an order that we should follow. We disregard nature, what reality is, and seek to create our own moral environment at great peril. And if we attempt to offer guidance without grounding our wisdom ultimately in Being, in reality itself, our efforts will fail fully to engage the human heart. Deep down men and women today yearn for a proper ordering of their lives, an ordering rooted in reality. People no longer see endless technological advances, helpful though they are, as the key to human fulfillment. The unrealistic optimism of modernity's promise has been tempered, in part by the perceived danger of a world that seems less stable and more disconnected from authentic human values. The time has come for many books to be written from a more classical perspective, a perspective that seeks real knowledge of *what is* as an integral part of understanding *what ought to be.*

CHAPTER I

THE VOCATION TO FATHERHOOD

*All Fatherhood Has Its Source in God, Who Has
Built It into Each Man's Nature*

All fatherhood is ultimately rooted in the fatherhood of God, who perfectly governs and cares for his world and his children. God's act of creation is a supremely fatherly act: He calls into existence from nothing all that is (besides himself), endowing each particular being with its own nature and purpose, each reflecting some aspect of his more perfect Goodness, Truth, and Beauty. There was no need for God to create; He is the fullness of life and perfectly happy in himself, a Trinity of Persons and one God. This is so much the case that it can be said that God plus his creation is not greater than God himself.[2] God created to communicate his own goodness to others, for the simple reason that goodness is diffusive and seeks to share life with others. And thus all creation is both God's free gift and his own domain, perfectly under his providence and governance.

Likewise, after we sinned, his supreme act of redemption shows the extent to which a true fatherly heart can go for the good of others: He sent his only Son to conquer sin and establish an even more perfect work of grace, a higher union between humans

---

2. Robert Sokolowski makes this point in his excellent book *The God of Faith and Reason* (The Catholic University of America Press, 1982). He calls this "the Christian distinction," a distinction that was not recognized by the ancient Greek philosophers. He shows that this distinction came forcefully into Western thought through St. Anselm, a point often missed in critiques of his ontological argument.

and God, more perfect than if humanity had not sinned and soiled creation, apparently spoiling God's plan.[3]

So God is the source and model of all fatherhood. It is not that our human institution of fatherhood can be used to establish an analogy by which we can try to understand God. This proceeds backwards. Fatherhood is not something human that we then use to speak imperfectly about God. No, fatherhood is perfectly present in God and analogously present among men.

Those who argue that we need different language to talk about God when working with those who have grown up lacking good human models of fatherhood miss this key point. It is unfortunately true that some do grow up today not knowing any wholesome examples of true fatherhood, seeing only the abusive and unfaithful side of men. This does not, however, negate the need for using the language of revelation to refer to God the Father, since it is by learning about the perfect fatherhood of God that people can begin to understand the fundamental vocation to fatherhood written on the heart of each man. This is how we begin to glimpse the reality of fatherhood that we have longed for in our hearts, knowing that whatever abuse may exist around us is not the truth about human love.

The vocation to fatherhood is built into the very nature of each man. Simply put, fatherhood is the vocation of a man to exercise dominion through service and to form others to participate in this mission. It is characterized on the natural level by a desire to govern and serve, along with others, in one or more domains where he has responsibility, whether in his own home and family, a particular community, a company, an institution, a team, a part of the land, or a particular job. In so doing, he serves others by providing for their needs, as well as educating his children and others so that they can likewise become providers and protectors, continuing and

---

3. And thus the Easter Vigil liturgy sings in the *Exsultet* of the "truly necessary sin of Adam" as a "happy fault that earned for us so great, so glorious a Redeemer."

furthering his fatherly providence and governance. On a supernatural level, a man experiences his call to fatherhood as intimately connected to the education and formation of his children and others to ground their lives in the Truth, to follow God and his laws with an upright heart, to be on the path to becoming saints. Thus, we can summarize the elements of the vocation to fatherhood as threefold: to have dominion, to serve, and to pass on one's mission to others.

This vocation to fatherhood is common to all men, although in different ways. Most are called to marry and form a family, enter a particular profession, and exercise heroic and self-sacrificing virtue in their ordinary family and professional spheres. Some are called to exercise a higher paternity through forgoing marriage. Called to the priesthood or another single vocation, they exercise fatherhood over many, becoming the fathers of fathers.

Boys Growing into Men, the Awakening of the Desire for Fatherhood

As a boy grows into a young man, his desire for fatherhood, a desire built into his very nature, gradually matures. Signs of this awakening can be seen in the things boys enjoy, in their play, and in the types of stories that capture their imaginations. Boys again and again gravitate to the same sorts of things in similar ways. The Ancients would call this an expression of "teleology" or "final causality," and value it as important for understanding the nature of boys. Teleology or final causality emphasizes that a thing exists for a purpose and, especially in living things, that there is an inner-directedness toward certain ends built into its very nature.

One of the earliest expressions of paternal inclinations in boys is fort building. Building a fort is like establishing a homestead, a small kingdom where a boy is the lord of the manor. Young boys love to build forts, forming alliances with other children and welcoming them into the fort. I well remember my numerous childhood attempts at building tree forts of various levels and strange configurations. I recall my mother or father taking me to the local saw mill to buy a pick-up truckload of "slab wood"— discarded boards with tree bark on one side. We could take as much as could fit into a pick-up truck for five dollars. I used these imperfect boards to build weatherproof structures. To spend time in such a fort in a rainstorm without getting wet I considered a great victory.

The Heights School, an all-boys' school for grades three through twelve, and the institution where I'm employed, is an ideal place for lower school boys to build forts. The lower school is located in "The Valley," a wooded setting with log cabins as classroom buildings. Boys in grades three through five build forts, form alliances, and defend their territory in a rapidly changing political landscape. The forts are typically built of fallen branches, rocks, an occasional board, or any other material that nature provides. Some boys have even been known to bring additional materials from home, a practice the faculty generally discourages. There are no classes on the art of fort building; the lower school teachers rarely get involved unless there is a problem in need of adult intervention. Even so, every year each new group of boys spontaneously engages in this activity during recess. It is in the nature of boys to do this.

My own sons have constructed various forts in our small wooded backyard, in suburban Washington, DC. From an early age they have asked for their own sets of tools and have used them to build tree forts and dig holes for underground forts, prompting me, and especially my wife, to worry about not only safety but how our backyard looks to neighbors. We have, therefore, formed a "parental zoning and permitting department" that over the years has become increasingly difficult for our young petitioners to deal with. New construction projects must have detailed "architectural" plans before parental approval will even be considered. When my two oldest boys, Michael and Thomas, were young, they dug a hole so deep that one would climb into the pit and scoop dirt into a bucket which the other would pull up and empty. When they decided to start "tunneling" sideways I knew this project had to end for safety reasons.

For boys, fort building and similar types of play display a drive to join with others in forming a domain, a small kingdom, a homestead of sorts. As a boy matures, he realizes that he could become a man who establishes his own family and home and defends it from outsiders. When my daughters have gotten involved in these activities—and they seem to enjoy it every bit as much as my sons—they typically add a feminine touch, sometimes "decorating" the fort or bringing household items into it.

Stories of pioneers and settlers resonate with the natural longings of boys. Common boyhood interests like hunting, fishing, and gardening, as well as chores like collecting firewood, carpentry repairs, and landscaping are connected with this growing paternal sense, as the growing boy considers what would be involved in taking care of others, particularly his own family. Backpacking and camping trips appeal not only to a boy's healthy sense of adventure but also indirectly to his growing sense of paternity: can he carry what he needs to survive for a few days and thus show his ability to forge his own way in the world as one who knows what is involved in taking care of himself and others?

In young boys these budding paternal movements have very little to do with girls. Typical healthy boy interests reflect a desire for independence and freedom, staking out a domain and governing it, and showing that one can face the world and secure what is needed. They are not yet interested in involving girls in this process as potential future partners in establishing a home. While driving, a mother of boys at my school once heard her two grade-school boys talking about girls in a peculiar way. The conversation went something like this. Said one, "I don't think I could do it. I don't think I could kiss a girl." Replied the other, "I think I could do it. I think I could kiss a girl if she would stay with me and help me take care of our home and she was a good cook."

As a boy becomes a young man, the wonder of God's plan for human love will unfold before him, provided obstacles do not get in the way and he is given the right mentoring by his father. He will come to recognize the beautiful complementarity between men and women, seeing that God's plan for human love is based on a male and female relatedness that God has built into human nature. God created Man male and female, establishing an orientation to relation in the very fabric of their beings. Youthful fort building and a liking for adventure stories about boys and dogs in the wilderness mature with recognition of the added dimension of human love intimately connected to the wellsprings of life.

CHAPTER 2

PREPARING FOR MARRIAGE

Selecting a Spouse

If the call to marriage grows in a man's heart, if God opens up this path before him as a real possibility to follow, he will need to consider whether his professional and personal situations are compatible with entering into marriage. A man should only date a woman if he is ready to be open to the vocation to marriage, with all this entails. If, for some reason or other, he is not currently ready to enter into the state of Holy Matrimony, he simply should not form an intimate personal attachment to a woman. Instead he should focus his efforts on removing whatever impediment exists to his following his vocational calling from God. Growing close to an attractive woman can lead to only two possible outcomes: the natural completion of this relationship through the marriage union or a potentially painful break-up. If someone is not ready (or at least close to ready) for the first outcome to be a possibility, then such a relationship most likely will not end well. It is possible, but difficult, for a couple to slowly develop their relationship over the course of several years. I know happily married couples who were high school sweethearts, dated through the college years, and only married after that. This is very difficult, however, and is not what typically happens with high school romances.

Built into God's plan for married love are powerful emotions that move a man's heart toward a particular woman. These emotions are good and help men see the great goodness of the vocation to marriage. But it is important that these passions be integrated fully into one's personality rather than simply blindly followed. Ideally, emotions should be under the governance of reason, not in order to suppress one's feelings but to purify them and direct them toward the greatest good.

It is thus important for a man to think carefully about the qualities that are important in the woman he intends to marry. He should not "fall blindly in love" but rather keep possession of his heart, protecting its integrity and making a conscious decision to give it to the right person. An old saying captures part of this truth: "Do not marry a woman who is so beautiful that she bewitches or so ugly that she causes twitches." While there is certainly wisdom in this earthy, practical advice, for one who guards and governs his heart it would not be a problem to marry the most beautiful woman possible, so long as she is good.

With this in mind, a man should rationally ask himself several questions about his potential spouse and carefully consider the qualities that are important for his lifelong partner to possess. A few of these questions are:

- Do I share common interests, including intellectual interests, with this person so that, when the emotional part of "falling in love" subsides—as it must from time to time, even for long periods—we will still enjoy each other's company?
- Does this woman have a strong character? Is she capable of making a lifelong commitment and sticking to it even if things become difficult? If she has faced adversity in the past, how has she responded? Is she fully committed to her family as a good daughter and sister?
- Would this woman be a good mother to our future children? Would she be self-sacrificing and kind, yet not overindulgent? Would she give priority to her family or would she likely place a career or other concerns first? Is she open to having the children God wants to send?

- Would she help me grow in virtue? Does she have the strength and wisdom to correct me when I need it? Would she try to help me become the best man I can be, encouraging me to improve?
- Is she committed to the Truth and to following God's way? Is she a woman of prayer? Would she be a strong partner in passing on the faith to our children and others?
- Is she herself open to corrections when she is wrong? Does she always have to have her own way or is she willing to compromise? Does she have the humility and other virtues necessary for being the heart of a family? Does she have a sense of humor?

It would be a mistake to think a person must be perfect already (as the above questions may imply) before she can be the right one to marry. Marriage is a great path to holiness, to real sanctity. Nobody entering marriage is perfect already, and it is God's plan that through the joys and challenges of married life spouses gradually grow closer to the full image of Christ and his bride, the Church. So a man should not expect perfection in his future spouse, just as an honest look at himself will reveal that he also is a work in progress. Even so, there is a great difference between the character of someone genuinely striving for holiness, for growing closer to God and his ways, and someone whose fundamental orientation is elsewhere. Without suppressing or disregarding one's heart, it is important to give careful rational consideration as to the traits important in the person one is considering for marriage.

Courtship Today

If a young man is ready for the possibility of marriage and believes that God is drawing him toward this path, he is ready to begin to court a woman who could be his wife. The traditional norms that governed courtship in previous generations have largely disappeared from contemporary culture. While there are still certain recognized manners and customs, the loss of most of the more formal norms of courtship have left young couples in a difficult position. They have a great deal of freedom to determine for themselves how they will spend time together as their relationship deepens. This freedom can be used well and for the good, but it certainly requires some careful reflection as to what is best.

Traditionally, a relationship between a young man and a young woman existed in the context of family and community relationships. Within the community there were organized events, such as formal dances with dance cards, which helped young men and young women become acquainted according to certain set patterns. While close attachments certainly formed, especially in unguarded hearts, the overall formal structure of these events encouraged a sensible reserve. And it was common for a young man and a young woman to get to know each other's families and to know the other in the context of his or her family. It is still common for a man to ask the father of the woman he wants to marry for permission to propose—one of the few vestiges of a traditional approach.

Today, particularly on college campuses, relationships develop without this traditional context and support. College students develop relationships largely without reference to their families and societal norms. Their peer group provides a quasi-familial context, but the relationship between two young adults develops for the most part in a direct and unmediated way. In such a situation, it is easy for a level of intimacy to develop quickly, presenting both physical and emotional challenges. Young adults who are aware of this potential problem will look for opportunities to temper the relationship so it does not develop too quickly. They will realize that it is healthy for each of them to spend time with other friends and to have interests pursued apart from the other. They will also look for ways to contextualize their growing relationship into broader family and societal relationships, getting to know the other's family sooner rather than later for example. Rather than just spending unstructured time together, they will look for opportunities to engage together in worthwhile cultural or even service-oriented activities.

In spending time with his potential future wife, a young man will naturally grow in his affection for her. As he comes closer to discerning the vocation of marriage with a particular woman, it is good that he grow in love for her, a love that will be strong and passionate. Part of what draws a young man to marriage is the powerful attraction God has built into his nature toward the woman whom he recognizes as "bone of my bone and flesh of my flesh," as completing him in some way. God's plan for married love is profoundly good. A young couple in love feels drawn to the goodness of God's plan for married love.

As with all goods of this earth, however, the human heart can attach to what it desires in the wrong way, trying selfishly to own and use the other, rather than following God's plan as known by one's reason enlightened by faith and grace. There is a primacy to the interior struggle—to allow the heart to form an attachment only to a certain extent, as dictated by right reason and a settled decision to respect the fact that the human heart is ultimately fulfilled only in friendship with God. Consequently, specific guidelines also should be followed when he is with this woman.

When with a woman, it is the man's responsibility to avoid any type of contact that leads to sexual arousal. A man can be easily moved through what he sees and through the sense of touch. A true gentleman will find a way politely to remove himself from a situation where his passions are excited. To give into the pleasure of arousal outside of marriage is a serious abuse of God's gift of human love between a man and a woman. The motions of the heart and body are meant for the marital union of husband and wife. Any other use is contrary to their nature, to God's plan for human love.

Guarding one's heart and saving it for marriage is very much an interior reality. But this interior reality is supported by practical and specific ways of relating to the other person.

Practical Concerns

A man is ready to enter into the vocation to marriage only if he is prepared to shoulder the responsibilities of raising a family and possesses a level of maturity, a strong character, and a heart open to growing as a husband and father. The couple must also be in a position to be able to support a family financially. Typically, this means the father has a stable job that is adequate to support a family if his wife decides to stay home to take care of young children either full- or part-time. Sometimes, for practical reasons, the husband is the one who stays home or only works part-time while the family is primarily supported by the full-time work of the wife. When children are very young, it is best that they have the direct care of their mother as much as possible. While a father can do an adequate job in this area, he cannot fully provide the nurturing that a mother more naturally provides. The best thing for a baby is to be breastfed, if possible, by his or her mother in the early months.

Being in a financial position to welcome children does not mean the couple needs to be wealthy. They do not have to have a perfect house, or large savings, or to have worked out how they are going to pay for their children's education. It is perfectly reasonable to start marriage in relative poverty, with a simple apartment, an old car, and a job that does not allow for the couple to put away significant savings each month. There is something beautiful in identifying with the Holy Family in this way. Just as St. Joseph supported Mary and Jesus by his simple profession as a carpenter in Egypt and Palestine, so a father need only to have a simple profession today, one that can support his family in their basic needs. Even for those who have more lucrative work, there still will be challenges and hardships, perhaps including illness, loss of work, or even particularly difficult external events in their community or nation. None of this is new. Throughout history, numerous Christian families have faced significant hardships with a humble spirit of trust in Divine Providence. And even in those cases where things did not work out, for example, where family members were lost to war or disease, heroic men and women have placed their ultimate trust in God, not in this world, and have been more than amply repaid.

It is important that the married couple be ready to welcome children from the beginning of their marriage. In some rare cases it could be acceptable to delay welcoming children for a short time through morally licit means, such as natural family planning. This is far from an ideal situation, however, and prolonging it can harm the couple and their vocation to marriage. To stifle the fruitfulness of married love from the start of married life introduces a strain into the relationship. Generally speaking, if a man and a woman are not ready to welcome children, for whatever reason, they are not ready to get married. There may come a time later in their marriage when it is best to delay welcoming more children for a period of time or perhaps for the remainder of their fertile years. Hardships that require this do come up—things like loss of job, serious illness, or even serious mental strain on the part of the husband or wife. In these cases, the couple can practice natural family planning without regret and with hope for relief from their present difficulties as well as prayerful trust that God will provide such relief if it is his will.

CHAPTER 3

THE FATHER AS HUSBAND
OF HIS WIFE

"Husbands, love your wives, as Christ loved the church and gave
himself up for her, that he might sanctify her. . . ."
(*Eph 5:25–26a*)

Except for his relationship with God, no other relationship is as important for a married man as that with his wife. His priorities should be God first, his wife second, and all other human relations and concerns, even his children, subordinate to these priorities. Fortunately, these different relationships, far from being in opposition to each other, are typically compatible, and a man is best able to give what is needed to his wife, children, and others when his life is ordered in this way. If it is clear to his children that he loves and cherishes their mother, they will feel a deep sense of security, knowing their very existence is intimately connected with their parents' love.

The children may at times try to vie for the attention of their father or mother in a way suggesting that they want to be more important to a particular parent than his or her spouse is. This is not unusual. But if the parents reply with a firm and loving message that there are behavioral expectations and clear boundaries, and that it is perfectly reasonable that Mom and Dad structure family life to provide time for each other along with time with their children on their own terms, then the children will internalize this structure and feel secure in it.

Being a good husband to one's wife entails many things: sacrificing oneself and one's wants for her good; praying for her; guarding one's heart only for her, both at times when affection for her comes easily and spontaneously and at times when the heart is dry in its affection for her; spending time with her; listening to her; supporting her in the things she wants to accomplish; opening one's heart, including one's struggles, to her; and now and then concretely showing one's love for her, whether by flowers or a gift or whatever it may be. This is a matter of interior dispositions—of having one's heart sincerely devoted to her, even if this is displayed by an act of the will that goes against one's emotions at the time—as well as exterior actions. A woman almost always knows, by a "sixth sense," if her husband's heart is divided. He will not be able to hide the divided condition of his heart by doing things she wants, like helping with housework. It is nearly impossible for a husband to go through the exterior motions without the wife knowing if his heart is divided in its loyalties.

Shortly after we were married, Angela and I were talking with some of my relatives at a family gathering. My aunt asked me how our early months of marriage were going. I replied that all was well now that I had learned the lesson of "Angela time." This reply brought amused looks and then many laughs as I explained what I meant. I related how confused I was at the end of a day, in which Angela and I spent time together doing many things, to hear her say in an accusing manner something like, "We don't really spend time together anymore," as I started to read a book. I would answer that we had been together most of the day, had run errands together, had worked on tasks together, and that I did not understand her statement. But gradually it dawned on me that Angela meant that, although we had spent time doing things together, we had not spent time focused on each other. I came up with a name for such focused time: "Angela time." "Angela time" is basically time when we are not busy doing something else and I am listening attentively to her talking about her day and what is in her heart while she does the same for me. I also had learned that it would be a mistake either to talk or joke too much, not listening with my undivided attention, or else not to talk at all, giving the impression I was not interested in her.

Sometimes a husband might complain that he cannot please his wife because he will get in trouble for either talking too much or too little. Although it may seem this way at times, what a wife typically expects is perfectly just. She demands that her husband's heart be directed toward her, that he cherish her, that he respect her, that he love her, and that this is shown in how he behaves when he is with her.

This can be confusing to men because they are typically content to do things with their friends. This focusing on doing something with the other is quality time for a typical man. Women, while also appreciating doing things with their friends, need time set aside specifically for the relationship. Angela enjoys working on projects with me. But she also needs some time when we are alone and can talk. Although she does not need lots of "Angela time," the difference between having a few minutes during the day to connect and then some more time in the evening, and not having this time, is quite significant. I now realize that omitting "Angela time" is akin to placing the "agenda" or "the schedule" ahead of her. A wife has an amazing ability to know when her husband's heart is divided, when he is placing other concerns ahead of her.

Men typically value "the schedule" or "the agenda" while women, without neglecting these things, place a higher priority on relationships. Reflecting on this, we see another dimension of the miracle at the wedding feast at Cana, where Jesus turned water into wine at his mother's prompting. First of all, it was Mary who noticed that the host family was likely to be embarrassed by running out of wine and this could damage relationships. Bringing this gently to her Son's attention she is met with a typical male response, "It is not my time." By this Jesus meant that to perform this miracle at this time would advance the schedule of his public ministry, leading him to begin this phase of his life sooner than anticipated and ultimately leading sooner to the cross. Mary would have none of it. Her way of accomplishing both miracles, the changing of the water to wine and the changing of the schedule of her Son's mission, was full of love, common sense, and piety mixed with taking charge. Turning to the servants, she clearly considers the problem solved and gives instructions, "Do whatever He tells you to do."

Practical Steps

While it is a fundamental priority that a man directs his heart toward his wife, this should lead to concrete acts of service. It is not enough simply to have one's heart turned toward one's wife if love is not shown in actions. And while different women like different things, the following are some commonly appreciated acts of service and expressions of love.

- **Bring her flowers.** There are times when this is expected, such as Valentine's Day or perhaps on her birthday. But giving flowers on a seemingly random day, out of the blue as the expression goes, can show one's love even more powerfully. To give her flowers on her birthday, when they are expected, is a good thing; to give flowers on an unexpected day with a note that says you could not wait until her birthday to show how much you love her, can go even farther.
- **Help with some household chores.** In most homes, some sort of division of labor naturally emerges. Usually it is not as pronounced today as in former times, when men and women had mostly distinct and complementary jobs that needed to be done to run the farm and homestead. Men would be more likely to do the tasks requiring the most physical strength such as plowing the fields with a team of oxen, while women were responsible for the domestic tasks involved in making the house a home. Running a modern household is different, and

the chores often can be accomplished equally well by men or women. Sometimes the division of labor is simply one of habit, an equitable arrangement whereby husband and wife both take care of aspects of running the household and appreciate each other's contributions. Even if the husband is doing his fair share of the work around the home—and he should—he ought to look for opportunities to help his wife with the work she does; she will appreciate a helping hand to make her work easier. And helping with the dishes or helping put away a load of laundry (especially if it involves carrying a heavy basket up stairs) can be a great show of appreciation and solidarity.

- **Take her out on a date on a regular basis.** In the ordinary hustle and bustle of life it can be easy not to schedule time specifically for being together. But this time is very important for nurturing the marriage relationship long term. While it is possible to get by with ordinary times of conversation throughout the day and especially in the evening, there is something different about a specifically scheduled time when husband and wife go out to enjoy a meal together, take a hike through the woods, visit a museum, listen to a concert, or any number of other activities.

- **Watch a romantic comedy with her.** When a typical guy wants to watch a movie, he may not naturally gravitate toward romantic comedies. But some women really like these funny romance movies and they can be enjoyed by both wife and husband. I really enjoyed the A&E version of Jane Austen's *Pride and Prejudice*. The dialogue between Elizabeth and Mr. Collins when he attempts to propose to her is nothing short of hilarious. And even if a particular movie is a bit on the dull side, it is still good to spend an evening watching a movie that she selects or you select with her in mind. But make sure that you do this cheerfully. No one appreciates watching a movie with someone who is obviously doing so reluctantly, as a mortification. And from time to time it is fine to see if she is up for watching that Civil War documentary or whatever most interests you.

- **Encourage her to go out with her women friends from time to time.** Most women have particular interests in which you simply are not going to be able to participate and still remain normal. Watching a romantic comedy together may be fine, but visiting a nail salon is going too far. Women also need to talk about certain things together that are best not discussed with their husbands. No man can reasonably be expected to listen to and participate in a discussion of the latest women's fashions or makeup and skin care products. So it is best, for both for you and for her, that you encourage her to socialize with her women friends once in a while. Just as men need to be able to talk with other men about things that most women are simply not interested in, it is important that your wife have opportunities to do this with her women friends.

- **Remember her birthday and your anniversary.** This point may be so obvious that it does not need to be made. Even so, based on the potential for forgetfulness on the part of the male sex, it is perhaps best to state it clearly. During the same family conversation when there was much laughter about "Angela time," my uncle shared a story of his own. He was recently married and did not know what to get his wife for her birthday. He asked her what she wanted, and she replied something like, "Don't worry about it. You do not have to get me anything." Unfortunately, he took his wife at her word and, perhaps reasonably in some sense, did not get anything for her birthday. When the day came, she patiently waited for him to surprise her as the hours passed. When it was time for bed and it became clear that he did not get her anything—which to her was basically equivalent to not "remembering her birthday"—she let him know about his deficiency in no uncertain terms. His humble protest that she said she did not want him to get her anything was decisively rejected. How could he be so thickheaded as to think that she actually meant what she said? Fortunately, this argument quickly passed, and my uncle and aunt can laugh heartily about the incident today.

- **Encourage her to pursue an interest.** Especially if your wife is a homemaker by profession, it is important for her to have some other interest to pursue. This may be a hobby that she particularly enjoys, an academic interest, or some cultural enthusiasm. It is healthy for any adult to have a particular interest outside of his or her normal work, both for enrichment and as a way to focus occasionally on something other than one's normal professional work. This is even more true when someone has a profession that requires constant dedication, as a mother of young children does who rarely leaves the home and only infrequently enjoys adult conversation. This means you will have to sacrifice some of your time to help your wife attend that class or do whatever else it is that enriches her.

This may sound like quite a bit for the husband to keep track of, and in some sense, it is. But it should not be a source of stress and concern to a young man considering the vocation of marriage. A woman who understands a man's nature will have reasonable expectations. A wife can tolerate many foibles and insensitivities from her husband, so long as she knows that she has that prized place in his heart. She will even readily forgive or overlook some fairly large mistakes or omissions. This is especially true if she sees her husband striving to grow and improve.

A man, who in some respects goes out of his way to try to show his love for his wife and serve her, will find himself so strongly in her good graces that she will go out of her way to serve and care for him in turn. It really is an amazing dynamic, one that is paradoxically both easy (when the man's heart really is turned toward his wife and he shows it, even if just a bit) and nearly impossible (when the man is distracted and taking his wife for granted, which she cannot help but notice). I think this dynamic underlies G. K. Chesterton's observation that polygamy makes no sense because being married to one woman is like being married to several different personalities all at once, or as Chesterton actually puts it, "Variability is one of the virtues of a woman. It avoids the crude requirement of polygamy. So long as you have one good wife you are sure to have a spiritual harem."[4]

Some authors even go so far as to describe the male-female tension in marriage as analogous to a continual state of war. C. S. Lewis humorously refers to this analogy in his book *The Horse and His Boy* when he describes Cor and Aravis's relationship as becoming so constantly confrontational that they decided to marry. Lewis writes, "Aravis also had many quarrels (and, I'm afraid even fights) with Cor, but they always made it up again: So that years later, when they were grown up they were so used to quarreling and making it up again that they got married so as to go on doing it more conveniently."[5]

The variability that Chesterton describes and the battles it sometimes produces, as Lewis states, can be a source of tension, but it also can be an opportunity for growth for both husband and wife. Love expands when partners appreciate their differences and find in them God's plan for individual and corporate growth in holiness.

There are certainly times when it is necessary to give a loving correction to one's wife, just as there will be times when she will need to give a loving correction to you. This needs to be done with great care and with an adequate appreciation of your own failings and sensitivity to her situation.

---

4. G. K. Chesterton, *Alarms and Discursions* (New York: Dodd, Mead and Company: 1911), *http:books.google.com*

5. C. S. Lewis, *The Horse and His Boy* (New York: Harper Collins, 1994), 241.

CHAPTER 4

THE FATHER AND ORDER IN THE HOME

In each man lurks a tyrant waiting to come out. From time immemorial there have been men who have ruled their families by lording their authority over them. And there are still families today in which the father exercises his authority to impose his preferences on his wife and children, insisting that other family members do things his way and not adequately taking into account the overall good of the family and the legitimate concerns and struggles of others.

I am not thinking of abusive family situations where the father showers down physical and mental abuse on others, perhaps augmented by alcoholism, mental illness, or some other problem. These tragic situations do exist, and those who are in such families need a great deal of love, support, friendship, and at times a way to leave the situation.

I am thinking rather about the father whose fundamental attitude is selfish—wanting to order things at home according to his personal preferences rather than as a means to serve the common good of the family. A father should try to serve the others generously, intentionally giving in to the preferences of his wife, first of all, and from time to time even his children when their desires go against what he would prefer but are still in accord with what is objectively good for the family.

Even so, it may be that more fathers today have fallen into the opposite problem. They simply do not exercise their authority, or else very rarely exercise it, perhaps only when there is a family crisis. The usual result is that disorder, at times bordering on chaos, reigns in the home. So, while there is a critical need for a father to strive to serve others, checking his potentially tyrannical male ego, a father, along with his wife, must also exercise real authority for the good of the family. Neglecting to exercise parental authority is perhaps the greatest abuse of authority in our time. If chaos reigns at home, it is likely traceable, at least in part, to a father's neglecting to exercise his authority properly.

Parental authority needs to be exercised to instill a constructive order and an atmosphere of peace in the home. It must be exercised constantly, at times directly but mostly in an indirect way, in establishing unspoken rules and certain common procedures, all contributing to a strongly lived family culture. A father who makes his authority felt only in a crisis is more likely to have to exercise authority harshly. Crises tend to require strong and decisive action; when the father "puts his foot down," insisting on a particular solution to the problem at hand, he is less likely to give adequate consideration to all the options and perspectives. It may not be really possible for him to do so and still take the decisive action needed to resolve the crisis. But this does not excuse the neglect of exercising authority that may have led to the crisis situation in the first place.

Not all crises can be prevented by the order resulting from a father's right exercise of his authority, but many can. Correct preventive measures are often effective in heading off more serious future problems: "A stitch in time saves nine" and, "An ounce of prevention is worth a pound of cure." I would go so far as to say that if the father properly exercises his authority, his home will typically be an orderly place full of peace and joy.

The Meaning of Order

Order in the home is not just material order, in which everything is picked up and put in its proper place. Material order does matter;

it is not good if clothes, toys, and other items are routinely left out of place, perhaps scattered on the floor or left on a counter or shelf where they do not belong. But to treat material order as the most important thing is to miss the whole point of order. Order is not an end in itself, something merely for appearances, like the order in museum exhibits. The purpose of order is to establish the conditions for proper action, for being able to develop oneself and serve God and others. Order multiplies one's time, allowing one to get much more done and, even more importantly, to get the right things done. Important as the external aspects of order are, then, on the most fundamental level order is an interior reality, a virtue, a good habit typically fostered over time and absorbed from one's environment.

The most significant expression of order is having one's priorities straight, which for a father is: God first, family second, and professional work as a way to serve society third. Within his family, the most important relationship is with his wife, for it is from the loving union of husband and wife that the children receive most of what they need from their parents. Since a well-lived family life also includes relationships with other families and friends, I prefer to think of the important network of social relations that make up life as also part of the second level of family life. Friends whom he knows through his professional work would fall within his third level of priorities so long as the relationship is mostly a professional one. To the extent that these friends and their families grow close to him and his family, however, they can take on a higher level of priority in his life. Aristotle noted that a true friendship, where the friends seek what is objectively good for each other, requires a close relationship that develops through living out the circumstances and events of life over time. Thus it is not possible for a man to have more than a few such close friends, and his best friend in the full sense of the word should be his wife.

God First

A father who possesses the virtue of order has practical habits in place to ensure that God really is first. These practical habits are what some call a "plan of life." Besides drawing his heart and mind to God frequently throughout the day, in the midst of his family life and work, he also sets aside specific times for God. Perhaps he says the Rosary every day, spends some time reading Scripture and other spiritual books, devotes time to mental prayer or other specific acts of piety, and tries to attend daily Mass when possible. Whatever the specifics of his situation, he should have a daily plan for placing God first by allocating time to fostering this relationship.

Friendship with God is first of all a work of God's grace, something only possible as a response to his loving us first and supporting us at every step of the way. But this does not mean we should wait for God to "touch our hearts" before we turn to him, as if living a Christian life meant wandering in a pious fog as an excuse for never really giving full attention to the One who loves us. How we are feeling is not the most fundamental thing. The battle of Christian prayer is lived by our turning to God while knowing full well that we could not do even this if not first drawn by his grace. But He wants us to respond to the grace that He very much wants to send. Far from being Pelagian, striving to follow a plan for one's spiritual life is the proper response of one who knows he is a child of God. In following a plan of life, one is responding to his loving Father by turning to him throughout the day, knowing that one needs to rely on his grace. And even if he does not feel anything, it is more than enough to know by faith, itself an infused gift, that God is looking lovingly on his little child, who is so aware of his dependence that he continually turns to him as a humble beggar seeking the gifts of prayer and grace. The first step for properly exercising authority and fostering order at home is for a father to place God first with a concrete plan of life.

Family Life Second

A father's heart and mind should be turned toward his family. He should consult with his wife, reflecting with her on their family life and the workings of the home. Spouses find natural times to discuss these matters, such as over a morning cup of coffee, during a shared car ride, or in the evening before going to sleep. A husband should have a well-developed habit of consulting his wife. Just as a good professional knows when to consult others in the office regarding decisions to be made, a husband should know when it makes sense to discuss some matter with his wife first. But since family life can become quite busy, and calm and reflective moments can become rare as children multiply, it is very helpful for husband and wife also to have scheduled meetings from time to time. As with good business practice, so these meetings should be planned ahead of time and approached with a certain amount of professionalism. Both husband and wife should prepare for these meetings, at least mentally and perhaps by writing down some ideas as well.

The agendas for these meetings will include such topics as:

- **Relationship between husband and wife.** Husband to wife: "Is there anything I can do to serve or help you better? What do you need from me?" The wife should be brave enough to ask her husband a similar question.
- **Children.** Consider each child and discuss how he or she seems to be doing. The insights of husband and wife often complement each other. Set goals for each child and talk about concrete steps to encourage each one.
- **Plans for the future.** Included in this category are such things as plans for professional work, possible family moves, major purchases such as a vehicle, general details of financial planning, and the desire of either husband or wife to engage in some form of educational or cultural enrichment. Particular topics will come up more or less frequently depending on the family situation.

- **Family calendar.** Almost every family has or should have some sort of coordinated family master calendar, either a physical one or an electronic version, shared between parents. It is necessary periodically to take a look at the different events on the horizon and rationally evaluate how full the family schedule is, if there is room to add other things, or a need to reduce commitments so as to protect family time at home. As children grow older and more numerous, the calendar becomes increasingly more complex, and it will be necessary to make many decisions about how well particular activities do, or do not, serve the needs of the family. Saying no to good activities, especially ones that children strongly desire, for the sake of the greater good of the entire family, can be difficult. Be strong in this area. It is ultimately in the best interests of the children to understand that they cannot do every good thing without impinging on the needs of the family as a whole. They will internalize this principle and come to place others' needs ahead of their own in the future.

- **Running of the home.** Here is the time to strategize on how best to foster the smooth running of the household. Does a particular area of material order need thoughtful attention? How is the chore plan for the children working? Are there time-saving methods that could be employed for the good of everyone? The father described in the delightful book *Cheaper by the Dozen* by Ernestine Gilbreth Carey and Frank Bunker Gilbreth, Jr. presents a rather eccentric but endearing model of efforts to improve family efficiency. He applies scientific motion study principles to everyday family tasks, timing different ways of doing household chores to determine the most efficient ones. Perhaps this book takes the goal of efficiency too far, but it does point to an important family concern.

- **Realistic expectations.** As the family grows, it is unrealistic to expect perfect material order all the time. The house will get messy. Young children will leave things out, and all members of the family from time to time will use things without putting them away. A good plan for family chores can help in this area, at least providing for a periodic tidying up when things are returned to their proper places. A cycle of messes and cleaning up, where parents and older children all pitch in to help, is a realistic expectation and goal. Trying to make the home of a large family with young children look like a museum, with continual material order, is unrealistic. Even if it could be done, it would probably be at the cost of stifling some other aspect of family life—for instance, discouraging or limiting children's imaginative (and messy) play or, even worse, encouraging them to waste time in front of mind-numbing screens.

The great advantage of holding regular professional meetings to discuss the good of the family and the running of the household is that it provides a setting for parents to discuss these things in a non-confrontational and rational way. Angela and I have found it helpful to do this away from the house, sometimes over dinner or a cup of coffee at a local restaurant or café. Ideally these meetings should take place on a regular basis, perhaps every other week or so. We usually fall short of this and end up meeting less frequently. Even so, the meetings are so effective that they smooth out many difficulties, equip us with a common plan of action, and prevent having to make hasty, spur-of-the-moment decisions. We really notice it when it has been too long since we last strategized together in this formal way.

A few words of caution apply here. Some individuals—and I think this is more likely the case with men—are particularly attached to their own ideas about how things should happen. The notorious male ego, which sometimes has its counterpart in women as well, can be a real source of blindness and tension. It is essential to examine oneself to make sure the parental meetings are not being used as a tool to exercise one's will over the other person. Pride is a dangerous vice to which we are all prone. And in marriage there is a danger that the pride of one or both of the partners will manifest itself in hidden ways, sometimes in the conviction that everything would be much better if the other person would only change in some way. If you approach a scheduled meeting with the hidden goal of finding a way to get the other person to change, you are wading into dangerous waters. A man should strive to discern how he can better serve his wife and family and what is objectively best for them. His attitude should be that he can best lead by doing more to sacrifice himself for the others, by being more generous.

But the danger of hidden pride and manipulation should not lead one to neglect to strategize with one's spouse for the good of the family, even pointing out with love areas where she can help better. If you notice your pride at work, thank God for this insight, pray for help to have the right motives, and keep moving forward. If you do not notice your pride, pray that you do (it's there!) and be brave enough to ask your wife how you can better serve the family and her. She will have some wonderfully helpful insights. To retreat into the comfortable option of letting things work themselves out, neglecting to exercise one's legitimate leadership and authority, in conjunction with one's wife, is the great parental mistake of our time. And it is a critical mistake resulting in weak families that lack what is necessary to survive and thrive in today's culture. Fathers who have tremendous professional lives, who are savvy and successful, who know how to interact with others in the business world, may neglect to apply these virtues at home. They can analyze a complex business problem and come up with a brilliant solution, but their home lives are a mess. They may come home and expect to be served in some small ways by their families but mostly to be left alone, able to kick up their feet and relax with a book or a show.

Practical Ways to Promote Order in the Family

If you and your wife are working together reasonably well as a team on the great adventure of raising a family, you are doing some of the most important things right. Here are a few other ideas for ordering family life for the good of everyone:

- **Post a daily schedule.** The night before is a good time to touch base with your wife in order to jot down a short plan for the following day and post it in a public place. This schedule should include appointments, planned activities, meals, and a few other structured times. A typical schedule for our family includes specific times for chores and also what we call "quiet time" (more below). In general, the more unstructured a day is, such as a weekend day or a vacation day, the more important such a schedule is. It can be difficult to get everyone started doing chores when they are in the middle of their own activities during free time. But if a family schedule is posted with definite chore times and free times, it is much easier and requires less parental energy to get the children to transition to chores. Children also tend to value their free time more and use it better when definite boundaries have been set for it.

- **Quiet time.** Children are by nature prone to activity. They typically move from one thing to another and may not stop to read or study on their own. But some quiet time reading and studying should be part of a balanced day. Children who take time out from their active play to spend an hour or so studying are typically happier and complain less about being bored. In our family, quiet time is usually about an hour long and we generally schedule one such hour of reading and study throughout the course of a typical weekend or vacation day. Babies and toddlers typically nap during this time. Young children who do not know how to read spend the hour drawing, working on an art project, or just resting. Young readers typically spend half the hour reading and the other half drawing. It is good for parents to insist that older children spend the entire hour reading and studying. I recommend periodically talking to each older child about his goals for learning new things. It is good to mentor older children in this area, helping them see that study should not just be a means for indulging the curiosities of the moment. Rather, one should come up with a reasonable plan to learn about something of value and interest. The goal is to spend this hour well.

- **Boredom.** Sometimes children complain to parents that they are bored or that "there is nothing to do." If this happens, I submit that you are doing something profoundly right. I once heard a wise person suggest that boredom is dangerous for children because it can lead them to go looking for trouble. There is truth in this: a bored teenager can find many distractions today that are not healthy for his or her soul. If, for example, your son or daughter is prone to wander freely through the Internet when bored, it is certainly a problem. But the problem is not with the boredom but with how the child is using his or her freedom (and with the parents who allow easy access to unlimited online content, perhaps by giving their son or daughter a smart phone). In normal situations a proper parental response to a complaint of boredom is something like, "You are bored. That's great! I can't wait to see what you will decide to do next." Boredom is a mild form of suffering that opens interior space for one to use his freedom to choose the good. It is a critical mistake to try to mask boredom with some mind-numbing activity, such as certain uses of screens. Boredom is an expression of a heart made for what is truly good, ultimately for friendship with God himself, recognizing that it is not satisfied with lesser things. Boredom helps a heart recognize that where it currently is, what it is currently resting in, is not enough. Children who are bored for a while end up deciding to engage in some type of quest, perhaps in the form of a new type of imaginative play. Many great quests and projects begin with unsettled children spurred into action by their boredom. A proper parental response to boredom is to cheerfully disregard the complaints or, if the complaints are becoming annoying, to assign some mundane chores. Some families have a chore jar that complaining, bored children must reach into to draw out a slip of paper with a chore on it.

- **Discipline of children.** Any parent will tell you that from time to time, even fairly frequently, young children need parental discipline. While a well-ordered home can reduce the need, it certainly cannot eliminate it. Children will misbehave, at times for attention, at times out of boredom, at times out of anger, at times because their overly developed sense of justice has been violated, and at times for a variety of reasons more or less baffling to the parents. Parents will employ various punishments, including perhaps the use of a form of incarceration often referred to euphemistically as "taking a time out" or even spanking. No normal parent relishes having to punish, but all of this is necessary, even if unpleasant. Parents should take encouragement from the fact that sound discipline helps establish healthy boundaries for children, boundaries that add to their overall sense of security and stability. It is terrifying for a child to experience reality as something he must define for himself, setting up his own rules and making decisions he is not ready to make. My recommendations in the area of parental discipline are fairly simple. First, when possible parents should consider the situation from the perspective of their child before acting. I realize that this is not always possible, as some situations require swift action. An angry boy chasing his sister with a stick needs to be tamed quickly. Second, parents should be understanding with childish mistakes but not with expressions of willful defiance. Willful defiance, including any direct challenge to parental authority or even a lack of respect to a parent, should be taken very seriously even if the matter that evokes the defiance is trivial. Parents generally should have a friendly rapport with their children, at times even playful and jovial. Even so, when a matter that requires parental discipline arises, the interaction needs to take on a serious tone that allows no defiance. Third, if a child cries in anger or dismay after being disciplined, send him to his room with instructions to cry into his pillow with the door closed so that he will not disturb anyone else. In fact, this is a great solution to any incessant crying or whining, so long as the child is old enough to understand and thus capable of controlling himself. I will sometimes tell my child that he can come out as soon as he is ready to be happy. It is very unpleasant to listen to children crying and parents and others in the home should not have to put up with it. After all, crying or whining is often just a more subtle means of defiance, a tactic children use to try to manipulate their parents.

- **Bedtime routine.** Every family has a bedtime routine that typically involves saying prayers, reading stories, having a snack, brushing teeth, and dressing in pajamas. These routines that seem to develop naturally in families with young children can also work well for older children. In our family, my wife handles most of the bedtime routine for the younger children, the ones who still mostly like picture books. I take the older ones to our study for prayers, a brief lesson, and then reading a few chapters from some well-chosen books. This is one of my favorite times in the day. The children sit around a table in our study and draw or work on puzzles while I read. This habit is so well established in our family that often our high school age children join in this special family time. Over the years, we have read and in some cases re-read hundreds of great books that I have enjoyed as well as the children.

- **Books or Bed.** This applies to the older children who do not have early bedtimes. "Books or Bed" is a specific time in the evening after which the children who are still awake are given an opportunity to settle down quietly and prepare for sleep.

The start time for Books or Bed can be written on the family schedule for the day or called on the spot as an exercise of parental authority. When Books or Bed begins, children must stop talking, playing chess, or fooling around and either do one of the few permitted activities or go to bed. The acceptable activities include reading, doing homework (computer use is only allowed for homework after books or bed has been called), working on an artistic project, and just sitting quietly and praying or reflecting on the day. On a school night, Books or Bed is typically called around 9 p.m., on a weekend night usually around 10 p.m. Some teenagers will stay up and talk into the late hours of the night if allowed. While it may not be a bad thing for siblings to enjoy each other's company, it is best that they have a period of time to prepare mentally for sleep and get to sleep at a reasonable hour. It is not healthy for children to have completely different schedules for school days and weekends. We have found that Books or Bed is the most effective way to help older teens maintain healthy sleep patterns.

The father's leadership role in his family

A father's leadership role in his family is exercised primarily by his active involvement in the life of the family, serving and guiding the others. This servant leadership role belongs to the father in a way peculiarly his, and he should not have to be dragged away from his professional life or other interests into family life by the admonitions of his wife. He should be involved in the life of the family, willingly investing his energy and time. Most of his leadership will be exercised in a natural way, simply by being involved and helping those around him.

He also should join his wife in thinking about the virtues and defects of his children and the running of the home. This involves applying the virtue of study to family life. While this is the responsibility of both parents, I think that the responsibility to take the lead falls in a particular way on the father, an insight that sheds light on those difficult and often ignored passages of Scripture that stress the primacy of the father as the one ultimately in charge of the family.

At times a father will need to lead by making unpopular decisions. This may even happen rather frequently with his children, as when he directs them to do chores. And traditionally the father has been seen as the one who has the final say about certain other things as well. If he is the one who is securing the family's place in the world through his professional work, some decisions in this area will naturally fall more heavily on him, even though he would be wise to consult his wife carefully. And to those who insist on the final authority of the husband in situations where there is an intractable disagreement between spouses, I only say that, while it may be necessary for a father to exercise this authority for the good in certain rare situations, it will be best if he never has to do so. This authority is like the alarm behind a glass pane with a hammer nearby and a sign saying, "In case of emergency break glass and pull alarm lever." When the glass is broken, a line has been crossed; and while a new pane of glass can be installed, the old one is gone for good.

Professional work and family life

Ideally, there is harmony between a father's professional work and his family life. It is best if he is able to model to his family a way of engaging the world, not merely to make a living, but to serve society and have a positive impact. But many pressures make this ideal difficult to achieve. Some corporate cultures expect long hours, a type of "marriage" to the job. A father may find himself in a situation where coming home for dinner on a regular basis could endanger his chances for promotion. Some fathers have heroically devoted themselves to working with such intensity and perfection that they have built up ample professional prestige and can leave the office earlier than their colleagues on a regular basis. The virtue of prudence, supported by prayer, is needed to know what is best to do in a particular situation. It may happen that for a time a father must be more absent from his family than is ideal.

The danger here, however, is that the father may come to think of his professional work as so important that there is no problem in shirking his responsibilities to his family in some ways. He may feel affirmed by the praise he gets for his professional performance. He may come to measure his worth by his professional status, which is a fundamentally disordered way of thinking. What should be firmly in third place, after the priority given to God and his family, has become his idol and takes the place of God and family for him. Yet if someone has a prayer life he is likely to see this happening. And one of the best means he has of rectifying the situation is turning to his wife to speak of his struggle and ask her for help and guidance. Even if she agrees that it is best for now that he continue to put in the long hours, the mere fact that he has discussed the matter with her will help to reestablish the proper order. If he does not neglect prayer, God will also provide the grace necessary for him to rectify his intentions.

In some cases, it is not the father's professional work but his wife's that is most important in supporting the family. Perhaps, in fact, because of illness the father is not even able to work outside the home and he may be entirely supported by his wife. Though there is a real link between professional work and the vocation to fatherhood, this is not always what happens. With a great deal of humility and trust in God, a family should embrace their situation, whatever it is. There is an opportunity even in the most difficult of situations for a heroic response with the help of God's grace. Those who accept their circumstances as God's will are given a way to go forward. Such situations are simply one more aspect of family life that a husband and wife need to study and pray about together.

There is no reason why a father cannot have a more direct role to play in the running of the household and the education of his children. The love in a true Christian family can more than make up for any difficulties that arise.

CHAPTER 5

THE FATHER AS TEACHER OF HIS CHILDREN

There is an easily overlooked but critically important task that every father should fulfill, namely, teaching his children about reality, teaching them the truth about what exists, what givens there are in the world. Teaching children about reality helps them form a complete worldview that is consistent and in accord with all perspectives, which will be a perspective open to faith.

It is not that fathers are consciously neglecting this duty, but it simply does not become a priority for most fathers, given all the other responsibilities they have. Fathers are usually the ones who have to provide for and protect their families. This often means long hours at a demanding job. It is also crucial that a father is a good husband to his wife, supporting her and spending devoted time with her each day. So it is not surprising that the father can easily fade into the background when it comes to the education of his children. After all, if a man supports and loves his wife, she will be so much better able to care for the children. It makes sense for a man with limited time to make caring for his wife a top priority. It is easy to see how a father ends up working very hard to support his family and care in particular for his wife, and as a result takes little or no direct role in the education of his children. This may be especially true of fathers who are confident that the education their children are receiving at home or in a carefully chosen private school includes solid faith formation and is in accord with the values of the family.

All of this is understandable but also a critical mistake, because nothing and no one can substitute for a father in the direct instruction of his children. Indeed, no other teacher is able to teach a wholesome, realistic outlook to children as effectively as the father. In the context of the modern nuclear family, this is even more the case.

If we reflect on the role of the father and his place in the family, we can see why he needs to teach his own children. A baby or young child typically experiences his mother as the one who nurtures and comforts him, in a sense almost as an extension of himself. The father, however, is "other." Even a father who is very affectionate with his children is still seen as a more mysterious figure, someone for whom the mother has a great deal of affection and whose presence immediately changes the situation. As a baby begins to become aware of himself and the world around him, he begins to see his father as the one who mediates the outside world to the family and to him in particular. Traditionally, the father is the protector of the family and the one who interacts most with the outside world, securing the family's place and its way of being there. As a child grows he naturally looks to the father to see how he should relate to the world and to all of reality. The mother is a sign and expression of the love and care of a family, of its "inside" or "interior life"; the father necessarily represents the family and its members in their engagement with what is outside and other.

Thus, a father mediates a vision of reality to his family simply by who he is and his outlook on the world. If he sees the world and reality only as a place where he must fight to secure benefits for the family, if the world for him is fundamentally a hostile place where those with the right street smarts can get ahead, then his children will naturally approach the world as an enemy, something to be conquered for gain. If he approaches the world as a place of danger, his children will naturally learn to fear reality. If he approaches the world as a place where one can find many pleasurable things, many forms of entertainment, then the children will view having fun as the purpose of life. And if the father views the world as fundamentally good as created by God (yet tarnished by evil and sin) and as such a wonderful arena for the great drama of the salvation of humankind, then his children will view themselves as joyful soldiers striving to become saints, fighting on the side of the underdog, which they also know is the winning side.

Since a father, simply by being a father, already mediates an understanding of reality to his children, he is, simply because of who he is as father, in a position to teach as no other adult can. If he sends his children to a school with teachers who support the values and faith that he and his wife share, then he does well. Yet, even the best possible school is always judged by a child in relation to the vision of reality he receives in a particular family, with the father's role being paramount.

If the father teaches his children about reality and especially about the Faith, he paves the way for his children to engage their studies in school and embrace the truth being taught there. On the other hand, to the extent he fails in this role, his children will not be as well situated to embrace the truth. And, if he never teaches his children and is seen by them as someone unable to speak with the authority of one who teaches, then the children are not likely to have a healthy interest in learning the truth about reality. The dominant paradigm for them in understanding reality is instead likely a reductive one, perhaps based on power and antithetical to the category of truth. Unfortunately, for many today belief is not firmly anchored in truth. Faith is seen as merely a source of comfort and family stability, not a radical proposition demanding a full commitment of self. Thus faith is easily rejected, especially when it is incompatible with immoral yet attractive life choices. The hedonism of our culture easily washes away a faith that is not supported by a consistent life, a faith followed merely out of social conventions and values not firmly rooted in the realm of truth.

Even more important than the actual lessons a father teaches to his children is what his act of teaching conveys to them. On the most basic level, a child naturally comes to value learning about reality simply because his father considers it so valuable that he takes time away from his other responsibilities to teach. The child thinks, "If Dad believes it is important that I learn about the world and my faith, then it must be really important."

A father's act of teaching operates on an even deeper level, however. A child sees that this man—a symbol of the outside world, of reality, of that which is "other"—is concerned with passing on the truth about this reality to him personally. And in teaching that he is subject to a higher authority, to God, this man, who has such power and authority, is naturally seen as participating in the fatherly providence of God.

Children quickly recognize that suffering is a part of human life. As they grow they also come to confront the limitations of one's particular place in the world as well as the fact of evil and the destruction and pain it causes. All of this serves to raise great questions: How am I going to navigate my way through this world? Is there meaning and purpose to my existence? Am I called to do anything particular? What is my vocation? Through the act of the father teaching the truth about reality, children come to see that, despite the apparent reign of evil, reality is fundamentally good, fundamentally within the control of God's providence, and as such the inheritance of the children of God. They see providential care poured out on themselves, not to erase the challenges of life's battles, but to help them find their way to strike the right blows for the winning side, a victory that will only be fully realized in the life to come.

Making the Time

Although, given other responsibilities, it can be challenging to find the time to teach one's children, fathers who are trying to care for their children know they must spend time with them. Even very busy fathers find ways to do that. It is not uncommon, for example, to see fathers on the sidelines of a sporting event, including fathers in business suits who have just come from work and have obviously made a conscious decision to spend the time to see their child's soccer game. Though it sometimes takes heroic efforts, many fathers are regularly, even nearly always, present for family dinner. And many very busy fathers reserve time on weekends, especially on Sundays, for their families and children.

The challenge then becomes for fathers to incorporate teaching into ordinary family life in a natural way, rather than struggling to schedule additional time for teaching. Different approaches can work for different families. Here are a few ideas:

- **A time for reading.** The evening, after dinner and before bedtime, is a natural time for a father to teach his children. Many families already have routines in which one or both parents read to children at this time. If a father gets into the habit of reading to his children, especially his older children, he can easily add a few thoughts on the well-chosen books being read. By choosing books that have a proper outlook on reality, whether literary works or saints' lives, the father can naturally become the most important teacher of his children.[6] This often works best in a place where children, especially the younger ones, have a table where they can quietly draw or work on an art project while Dad reads. The value is not so much that the father conveys a systematic body of information (the school does that) but that, in taking time to teach and learn with his children, he models an outlook on reality. There are many guides to excellent books that can appeal to children of different ages.

- **Creating the space.** The practice of family reading requires the elimination of distractions. Developing good habits of family life when children are young is a great help. Screens (television, video games, computers, cell phones) must be strongly

---

6. See the appendix for a list of some excellent books to read to children.

regulated by parents to create the "space" necessary for family reading. Having to compete with television shows will be a big obstacle. Limiting the influence of screens in the home is a necessary (but not sufficient) condition for a father to teach his children well. The contemplative nature of reading together is less appealing to someone who is accustomed to the intensity and pace of images on a screen. The desire for electronic stimulation can edge out appreciation of a spoken narrative. It is important to form children with a Christian view of time, namely that time is a treasure that we must sanctify. This rich view is not compatible with activities such as video games that merely "pass the time." Much modern entertainment is a practical expression of the nihilism prevalent in our culture, and wasting time implies that there is no meaning or significance to how time is spent.

- **Helping young children memorize.** If it is natural for a father to spend some time reading with his children in the evening, it will be easy to spend part of this time memorizing important things. I was surprised at how eager my children were to memorize, from lists (the Ten Commandments, the Works of Mercy, the Seven Sacraments, the Cardinal and Theological virtues), to important catechism questions and answers, and even common prayers in Latin.[7] It was not difficult to do. I say a line and the children repeat it. We go through the entire text like this about five times and then slowly say it together a few more times with me leading. The whole lesson usually takes less than five minutes per day, and it generally takes about a week for the children to learn something completely, although a review is needed periodically to keep this knowledge sharp. For example, while all the children could repeat the Ten Commandments independently after about a week of practice, neglecting to recite the Commandments for several

---

7. See the appendix for a list of things to memorize with children.

months thereafter was likely to result in forgetfulness. (Once someone memorizes something, however, it is much easier for him or her to memorize it again after it is forgotten.) Recently I was going through the corporal and spiritual works of mercy. My six-year-old daughter Lucy apparently conflated the two lists and, while thinking about the spiritual work of "praying for the living and the dead," announced the final corporal work as "burying the living and the dead." All of us, even Lucy, burst out laughing. Even though I know the chief benefit for the children is knowing that they are so important that their father is taking time to teach them personally, I can't help but be impressed by how much they actually have learned over the years. There is a theory of education promoted by E. D. Hirsch called cultural literacy that emphasizes the benefits of learning the terms, symbols, and stories of one's culture. Doing so helps people make sense of what they read and hear because they have a context in which to receive new information. Similarly, some good history teachers begin courses by having the students memorize a broad timeline for the period to be studied, so that they can better understand and place specific information in a context. My children approach classes in school with a basic knowledge already in place, some important vocabulary words, and a sense of what is true and good. This has helped them thrive in a school environment.

- **Brief talks or lessons.** In addition to ensuring that his children memorize some things that should be known by heart, a father should also from time to time give a brief teaching on some virtue or aspect of the faith or a proper outlook on reality. I find that this is best done as part of the lesson I give in the evenings around the time I read. Usually a brief talk like this takes the place of our five minutes of memorizing. The liturgical seasons offer a great opportunity for topics. The beginning of Advent relates well to the need to prepare one's heart for the coming of Jesus at Christmas by taking time out for prayer and doing acts of service for others. Christmas is a great time to talk about the Incarnation and salvation history. The coming of Lent is a great time to talk about sacrifices for others, prayer, mortifications, and penance. The readings at Mass also can provide opportunities for a father to address related topics. One word of caution here: do not let these talks be occasions for lecturing the children on how they should get along better and help more around the house. It is fine to bring up the virtues associated with cooperating and serving and even to mention the opportunities that family life provides for their exercise. The key is the tone—inviting the children to grow in virtue and in living their faith rather than pointing out deficiencies that are sources of frustration for their parents.

- **Educational projects with the family.** You and your wife can together plan projects to further the human and spiritual education of your children. During Advent and Christmas, a manger scene and other decorations in the home can enliven the imaginations of young and old alike. Angela places an empty manger that the children fill with pieces of yarn whenever they do a good deed for Jesus. On Christmas Eve baby Jesus appears, lying on this soft bed of yarn. Similarly, in Lent she puts out a baked "crown of thorns" with toothpicks as thorns. The children can pull out a thorn every time they offer up a sacrifice, which they are encouraged to do out of love for God. Also in this category are family service projects, such as visiting a nursing home. Great human formation can also come from visiting a museum, attending a concert or play, or even watching a select film together and then discussing it.

- **Family prayer.** Prayer in the home led by the father is an incredibly powerful witness to one's family and a source of tremendous family unity and strength. Some families set aside time every day, usually in the evenings, for prayers together. In our family we sometimes pray all together, for example, around the advent wreath or when saying a family rosary. On other evenings I say prayers with the older children as the start of our bedtime lesson and reading routine. Angela does the same with the younger ones, who typically go to bed earlier, while I read to the older ones in the study.

- **A sound philosophical foundation.** To be properly grounded in reality it is helpful to know something about metaphysics, the science that studies reality broadly considered. Metaphysics deals with the ultimate causes, and first and most universal principles of reality. Today, unfortunately, this science has been almost completely forgotten. Few people know much, if anything, about it. Some bookstores place their few metaphysics books (probably not about genuine traditional metaphysics anyway) next to books on New Age spirituality and the occult. I recently looked for a good metaphysics textbook for a discussion group and in the end had to order one I found from the Philippines. I am not aware of a good one currently in print in the United States in English. This deficiency is one of the main reasons for the prevalence of reductive and scientistic thought. Not knowing how to employ reason in a broad and expansive manner, many people seek truth only according to the methods of the empirical sciences. These methods are good and lead to some truth, but they consider only part of objective reality, leaving out considerations of form, finality, being, and essence to name just a few aspects of reality that are beyond the methods of the empirical sciences. Individuals formed this way have a difficult time recognizing and appreciating nature for what it is and finding accessible meaning in the created order that can serve as a guide to our efforts to follow a plan for our lives consistent with how we have been made. Fortunately, some people are aware of this problem and are working to rectify the situation. I would mention the work of Anthony Rizzi, specifically his *A Kid's Introduction to Physics (and Beyond)*, as well as many books by Peter Kreeft and Edward Feser. Part of metaphysics has been recovered by the classical education renewal in the form of Logic. A good text to begin with is Peter Kreeft's *Socratic Logic*. A few times each year, usually on vacations, I take my older children to the school at which I teach and cover some of this material with them. It is well received. Of course, most fathers are not professional educators and are not familiar enough with this material to do this well. We must all pray for the recovery of the full scope of human reason that Pope Benedict prophetically called for in his "Regensburg Address" and elsewhere. On a positive note, metaphysics has also been called the science of common sense. So, even though very few people today know metaphysics in a scientific way, many well-rounded and sensible individuals implicitly know much of this subject. Anyone for whom the works of J. R. R. Tolkien and C. S. Lewis resonate as true and important for our time is already well on his or her way to developing a strong metaphysical sense. This knowledge is infused at baptism with the gift of faith, but it is important that we give faith the full support of human reason rather than allow it to stand alone and naked against a hostile worldview.

- **One-on-one coaching.** As children get older, they become more capable of independent and self-directed work. A prudent father will welcome this development and adjust his mentoring role. A bit of personal attention to help his older son or daughter plan their studying can go a long way. This one-on-one conversation could take place at home or at a local coffee shop. The tone should be collegial, as both look at the big picture and what is the best study plan for a comprehensive development of one's intellectual life. Perhaps this will result in a plan to read some particular books, study a particular time in history with the help of a biography, work toward mastering a foreign language, deepen one's knowledge of the Faith, or even advance in math. This is a great opportunity to highlight our good fortune in being members of a free society where we can choose to pursue these goods, along with the danger of failing to use freedom for the good by not devising such a plan and so falling into an unstructured, unfocused manner of living.

- **Father and son talks.** A father's most important teaching responsibility toward his son is to help him understand God's plan for human sexuality. It is best that a father has a first talk on this subject with his son when he is fourth-grade age, although later (even as late as high school) is better than never. It is probably better not done at home. My own preference is a nearby park with lots of hiking trails. The father should explain God's plan for human procreation and the upbringing of children and let his son know that there are many evil forces raging against this beautiful plan of God. This is an opportunity to explain the virtue of chastity and the nature of the ascetical struggle for a clean heart. The session should end with the father telling his son that this is a very sacred matter that needs to be treated with discretion. It would be wrong for him to try to teach the intimate details of this subject to his friends, as this is the job of their fathers. Nonetheless, not all fathers know how important it is to talk about this with their sons, so it is possible that some boys will learn about human sexuality from other sources, many of which lack our understanding of the beauty of God's plan. If anyone starts speaking inappropriately about these matters, it is good to stand up for what is right, letting it be known that such talk is wrong and should stop. A father should end by encouraging his son to approach him any time with questions or ask a priest in confession. A chapter in this book is devoted specifically to preparing well for these important father-son conversations.

- **Father and daughter.** Another very natural yet powerful teaching opportunity is a father-daughter "date." This can be something very simple such as taking her out to lunch or for ice cream. No explicit teaching by the father on this occasion is necessary or even desirable. The mere act of taking his daughter out communicates to her that she is valuable and loveable and deserves to be treated with dignity. Every man who dates her in the future will be judged in her mind by how well he lives up to her image of her father. When a young man takes her on a date, she will know what to expect from him because she has seen the gentlemanly way her father has treated her.

CHAPTER 6

THE FATHER AS MENTOR
TO HIS SONS

To say parents are the primary educators of their children means more than that their authority should be protected and upheld. This is true, we should uphold it, and society and the government should respect the fundamental right of parents to make educational decisions regarding their children. But, more than an assertion of parental rights, the claim that parents are the primary educators of their children is a statement of the simple fact that from the earliest age children look to their parents to understand the world around them and their place in it. Parents mediate the world to their children, and a large part of how a child understands reality comes from his or her experience as a person in a family.

A clear example of this mediation is the indispensable and irreplaceable role of the father in the education of his sons in the area of human sexuality. A father's authority to teach is intimately connected to his living example as the father of his children and the husband of his wife, the children's mother. Simply because he is the father, his sons naturally look to him as a role model for the proper treatment of women, imitating how he cares for their mother and sisters. The father has a privileged position from which he can teach his sons about God's plan for human sexuality and fruitfulness, unfolding this topic in its proper context and full dimension. This is an area where a school is simply incapable of adequately assuming the father's role.

What follows are some practical considerations about how a father can educate his sons. They are partly based on my own experience with my older sons. And while this essay is specific to the father-son relationship, much of what is said also applies to how a mother could talk with her daughter. Ideally, it is best for a boy to talk with his father about these matters, and a girl with her mother. But where one of the parents is missing or unable to provide guidance the other must.

Getting the Right Message Out First

It is best to tell a boy about God's plan for human sexuality before he hears a version of it from another source. If a boy hears from his father first, other reductive presentations later will be less damaging. The boy will also be more likely to feel comfortable consulting his father later about anything that bothers him.

In times past, it was less likely that a boy would be presented with a deficient view of human sexuality at a young age. But today, even if a young boy does not himself view material that presents human sexuality inappropriately, some of his peers will probably have been exposed to it. Therefore, his first introduction to the subject could be in playground conversation with one of them. It is important that parents reach their children with the right message first, then reinforce this perspective throughout the formative years.

Parents initially convey the right message about human sexuality to their children through ordinary family interactions and through a few messages deliberately communicated in a natural way. Children see that their parents love and respect each other and that this love overflows to include the whole family. This good example is very powerful in conveying truths about human love.

A father can make this early formation of his children even more effective by verbalizing a few particular messages. He should tell them (more than just once) that he is very thankful to have met their mother, to have had this wonderful woman say yes when he asked her to marry him, and to be able to spend his life with her and the wonderful family that has resulted. In this way, a child will gradually see the unfolding of human sexuality in the context of a loving relationship between his mother and father, and will become aware that children are the result of the loving relationship between a husband and wife. The normal experience of human love, lived in a family and occasionally referred to, should be adequate for a boy up to about fourth grade.

The First Planned Father-Son Talk

Around fourth grade a father should have the first of a few planned talks on the topic of human sexuality with his son (and mothers with daughters, but that is another topic). I first spoke about sexuality with my oldest son, Michael, when he was in fifth grade. I told him that there was something I would like to talk with him about and set a day and a time. We drove to a nearby park with some trails that meander through the woods. As we started to walk, I told him I wanted to tell him about God's plan for human sexuality, that this is a very beautiful and good plan, and that it is under attack today by people who want to ruin it. He listened attentively and asked some questions which I patiently answered.

At the end of our discussion, I told him it is best if boys hear about God's plan for human sexuality from their fathers and that this happens for many boys. I also told him that some boys may not hear about this from their fathers but in other ways, which is not as good. I told him he should not be the one to teach anyone else about what we had discussed. Specifically, I told him that he was not to inform his brother Thomas, sixteen months younger, or anyone else at school. And I told him he needed to be strong in defending what is right in these matters; and if he heard anyone speaking badly about them, he should tell him to stop and, if necessary, inform me or another adult. He seemed to understand.

When we arrived home, Thomas was very curious. He knew Dad had left to have an important discussion with his older brother, and he wanted to know what it was about. He asked Michael several times, but all Michael would tell him was that he refused to talk about it—he would hear about it from Dad when the time was right.

This would not do for Thomas, so I agreed to take him out to talk with him. In going to the same park, walking the same trails, I had a similar talk with Thomas about a week later. Thomas was in fourth grade at the time. Since then, I have had similar talks with two more of my sons, Joseph and Stephen, when they were in fourth grade. At the end of each talk I emphasized that I was happy to answer any questions and encouraged my sons to feel free to come to me if they had any concerns in this area.

Following are some helpful points to keep in mind when getting ready to have a first father-son talk about human sexuality:

- **Begin with God.** Rather than saying "This is how babies are made," or "how human sexuality works," or even "I want to tell you about human sexuality," start with something like, "God has a beautiful plan for human sexuality that I, as your father, want to tell you about." All the impure lies about this topic are mixed with partial truths corrupted by a reductionism that considers part of the truth in a limited context. Referring to "God's plan" avoids this reductionism right from the start by setting the proper context. Once St. John Paul II was asked why so much art in the Vatican shows a great deal of the human body, including sexual organs. The questioner wondered if the Vatican was guilty of displaying pornography. St. John Paul II wisely answered that pornography is not pornography because it shows too much, but rather because it shows too little. He meant that there is no problem with showing the beauty of the human person through good art; the problem is reducing a person to an object, with his or her sexuality displayed in an objectified way. This pornographic objectification of the person can be done very effectively through suggestive clothing as well as by a lack of clothing. The essence of pornography is reductionism, not how much of the body is revealed.

- **Tell how you met your wife.** The story should be told as more than a simple lesson in family history; it should be told to make a few key points. Explain that as you got to know your wife you recognized that she is a wonderful woman with specific virtues (name some), someone you wanted to be with as a companion for life, and someone who would be a good mother. Gradually your love deepened, you decided to ask her to marry you, and she accepted your proposal. Point out that this is how families typically begin; that in God's plan a man and a woman meet, get to know each other, fall in love, marry, and are blessed by God with children. Note that children result from God blessing the marital love of a husband and a wife. The great goodness of God's plan for human sexuality will naturally emerge as you tell your story. Your son will understand how God builds into human nature the desire for marital love and a family, even as he sees it as a "grown-up thing" that does not yet relate to him experientially.

- **No need to get heavily into the mechanics.** An aspect of modern reductionism is inordinate attachment to efficient causality (which is only one of four types of causality, the other three being material, formal, and final) as the primary explanation of things. How a thing works is thought to be more or less everything there is to know about it. The mechanism of sexuality is not bad knowledge to have, and if your son asks questions about the mechanics, it is best to answer them. But a father's initial explanations should be more general and integrated into the full meaning of human sexuality, which certainly cannot be reduced to mechanical function. It is good to talk about how in God's plan a man and a woman fall in love and get married: that as a married couple they come together in the "marital embrace," that in this "marital embrace" there is a wonderful contribution by the man and a different but equally wonderful contribution by the woman, and that these contributions combine when a new human person is formed in the womb of the mother. Explain to your son that this new person begins very small and grows quickly. "Is it not wonderful that God makes a new baby come about through the love of a mother and father?" For older boys, it may be helpful to go into more details, even if not asked directly. The important thing to keep in mind is that this conversation should recognize the full meaning of human sexuality which is God's plan, and not reducible to a mechanical process.

- **Puberty.** A good way to open discussion of this topic is to tell your son a bit about how he will start to change in a few years on the way to becoming a man. Note the differences between boys and men, girls and women. I would put it like this: "Men have more hair on their arms and legs, bigger and more powerful muscles, and deeper voices; they need to use deodorant and shave. The passage to manhood is puberty. The changes take place over a few years and typically start in about seventh grade, earlier for some and later for others. They are very good and part of God's plan, although some things about puberty can be challenging. It is common for a boy to start to notice, even like, girls and women in a different way. Along with the changes in one's body there are changes in one's heart as well. God wants us to keep our hearts clean and reserved for love. Some people are called by God to do this through a celibate life, others through giving their hearts to one woman in the holy vocation to marriage. God could call you to either path, and you will be happiest if you pray to know God's plan for your life and then follow it when you see it. Because of sin, the human heart can be a traitor; it can seek comfort and fulfillment in things of this world rather than in God. The things of this world are good, as coming from God, but if we think only about them and forget that we are just passing through this life on the way to heaven, we will not be thankful and happy but covetous, anxious, and sad. Sin has wounded us, but God is there with his grace to help us when we turn to him. A small child may think he will be happy if he has a particular toy. But that toy does not make him or her happy for very long, and so we encourage the child to share, which is a good way to avoid becoming attached to things. When a boy going through puberty starts to notice girls in a new way, he needs to remember God's plan for human love. If it is his vocation someday to marry a wonderful woman, these new movements of his heart will find fulfillment in loving and cherishing a wife. In the meantime, it is important that he save his heart for this woman he will marry—or for a higher love if God calls him to celibacy. The virtue that allows him to do this is called chastity."

How long should this first father-son conversation be and how much should be covered? The answer is: it depends. If the first conversation takes place around fourth grade, there is no great need to cover things in depth. The main point is to have this conversation in order to give your son the right perspective before he hears other perspectives—as he will. The first conversation need not cover everything. Just present the basics in the right way; then let your son's questions guide how much further to go.

Ideas for Ongoing Father-Son Conversations

Other father-son conversations should follow the first. They may take place because a boy comes to his father with questions or because a father realizes that it has been a while since the last conversation and it is time gently to initiate another. It is to be hoped that a boy with questions about these matters will feel comfortable bringing them to his father. In many cases, though, he may be shy or embarrassed. A father can usually tell when it is time. If a year or two passes and all seems well, it still may be a good idea to have another walk with your son and ask if he remembers the earlier conversations about God's plan for human sexuality. Your son will appreciate your raising the subject and again speaking of the beauty of God's plan and the virtues that we are called to live. Following are points that could guide additional conversations (or, in some cases, could be brought up in the first father-son talk if appropriate):

- **Chastity.** Chasity is the virtue by which one possesses oneself so as to be able to love others with the pure love that God pours into our hearts. It is a virtue meant for everyone, married or single. A chaste person does not seek to use other people for his own benefit or pleasure. A chaste person can love in the best way possible because his loves are all in proper order. It can be a struggle to live this virtue. In talking with young boys, it is probably enough to let them know that we are called to have clean hearts and that if they have questions they can always ask their fathers, or ask a priest in confession. With older boys it can be helpful to talk about the practical side of striving to live chastity, how to "guard one's eyes" and "guard one's heart." A good illustration is the fall of the great King David, "a man after God's own heart." David's fall starts with his failure to guard his eyes. He looks at Bathsheba in the wrong way and one thing leads to another, culminating in the planned murder of Uriah. But David repents when corrected by Nathan the prophet. Talking about this story with your son can be a good way to teach about the struggle to live the virtue of chastity, as well as the healing mercy of God.

- **Modesty.** It is helpful also to mention modesty, one of the virtues that supports the virtue of chastity. Through modesty we live a natural refinement and elegance. Children should be told that not only should "private parts" be covered, but that one should dress in such a way that no part of one's body is inappropriately displayed. Boys should wear shirts, even on the hottest of summer days. Of course, a boy will not wear a shirt when swimming, but after leaving the water and toweling off it is best if he puts his t-shirt on just for the sake of greater modesty. Even if a boy sleeps without a pajama shirt, it is best if he wears one before getting into bed. Parents do well to explain these details as ways of living with more modesty, a word that points to the distinction between what is seriously wrong and what could be better.

- **More on puberty.** Before puberty begins, it is a good idea to tell your son about nocturnal emissions. My talks go like this: "The changes that take place in puberty are good, just like God's entire plan for human sexuality. One of them is that your body will start to produce semen. Semen is the part the father contributes to the new baby that forms in the mother's womb. The body produces semen in the testicles and the semen builds up to the point where it needs to come out. It can be a bit surprising when one has a nocturnal emission for the first time. This typically happens when sleeping and it may happen during a dream that you remember upon waking. It is also possible that you might not wake up during the nocturnal emission but notice when you do wake up that there are wet emissions in your underwear. It is not sinful to have a nocturnal emission while sleeping. On the other hand, trying to stimulate yourself to have an emission of semen on purpose is seriously wrong. This is called the sin of masturbation. It is wrong to stimulate oneself sexually either by some type of physical act or by using one's imagination. Not doing this is part of how one lives chastity, keeping oneself whole and pure so as to give oneself at the right time to one's wife or to offer this dimension to God alone if called to a celibate life. If you have questions about this, please feel free to ask me or a priest in confession."

- **We are warriors in a noble battle.** Educate your son about the battles that must be fought in our culture in defense of pure love. Remind him that the devil works by trying to corrupt something good so as to destroy it and turn souls away from God. I put it this way: "Given that God's plan for human sexuality is such a tremendously good thing, it is predictable that the devil should want to corrupt it. There are many examples of the devil's work in this area, including immodest pictures and videos that show people as sexual objects. The devil is the father of lies, and he is trying to spread lies about human sexuality. This type of material is called pornography. Pornography can range from really bad images (what most people think of as pornography) to more common images that also contain pornographic elements (even though most people do not think of these immodest images as pornographic) such as pictures on magazine covers in a typical supermarket. It is important to guard one's eyes and heart, and keep close to God through prayer and the sacraments. If you notice any of your classmates or friends looking at something they should not look at, you should tell them so. Tell them real men do not look at women like that and, if they would not want to imagine their mother or sister in that way, it must be wrong."

- **Empowering boys to be able to react strongly.** With my third and fourth sons, Joseph and Stephen, I added some additional instruction that was very well received. I told each of them that if anyone ever tries to show him a pornographic image on a phone, he should grab the phone and smash it as hard as he can on the ground, then stomp on it. Then he should tell the boy who had the phone something like: "If you have a problem with the smashed phone, tell your dad to call my dad." Realizing that I was serious, each son grinned dangerously, and I saw that he was hoping for a chance to smash someone's phone without getting in trouble. At this point I told him that I was indeed very serious, but he should only smash a phone if he was sure the image was pornographic. I have yet to get a call from a father or hear about any smashed phones.

- **Warriors are not victims.** The biggest danger about pornography is that it will stick to one's heart and mind. Children especially are vulnerable. They generally lack the capacity to deal with a situation in which someone tries to present them with impure content or situations. So, it is best if a boy hears from his father that he should take charge of the situation by rejecting this great evil in some way, whether smashing a phone, ripping a picture, or even screaming something like, "This is sick! Get away from me." In these ways a boy can actively reject impurity rather than be paralyzed by it. Child predators know how to exploit a child's vulnerability. They may leave inappropriate materials out for boys to "accidentally" look at, then follow up with them after they already feel compromised. Just as a knight draws his sword when it is time to fight the dragon threatening the castle, so we need to help our sons understand that there is a time for a violent and strong reaction against anything that presents women in the wrong way or that is perverse in some other way. A boy empowered by his father to fight in this manner will be much less vulnerable.

- **Knights defend women.** Part of the battle for purity is the defense and protection of women. Tell your sons that there is something very beautiful about femininity, and gentlemen should treat women with refinement and respect. Talk about good manners, such as holding a door for a woman or offering to carry a heavy package for mom. Make it clear that a boy is never to hit a girl. It is good to have a double standard at home in this matter. If one of your daughters gets angry and slaps one of her brothers, this should be addressed appropriately. But if one of your sons gets angry and hits his sister, it should be treated as a much more serious offense. Make it clear that it is never acceptable for a man to hit a woman.

- **Our Lady.** Encourage your son to have a tender devotion to Mary, perhaps under the title Mother of Fair Love. Turning to Mary for help in the area of human sexuality is tremendously effective. She defends those who turn to her and has a way of straightening out anything that is not quite right. Fathers also do well to invoke Mary's help before and while talking about human sexuality to their sons.

- **Never too late.** While it is best to take the proactive approach outlined here, reaching out to your sons before problems arise, it is also never too late. A father can still do a great deal of good by talking to his older son for the first time. Even in cases where healing and forgiveness are needed, a loving father reaching out to his son with encouragement can make the crucial difference. No matter how difficult the situation, God's mercy and healing are always possible.

Details at Home

Fathers should also make sure that practical preventative measures are employed in the home. But even though these things are very important, in no way are they sufficient to protect one's family. It would be a mistake to consider these steps as substitutes for father-son communication and trust.

- **Watch out for screens in your home.** All screens should be in public places where there is lots of family traffic. This is especially true for devices that can connect to the Internet. Many boys and young men are snared by Internet pornography simply by indulging their curiosity. This is much more likely to happen to someone privately viewing a screen.

- **Mobile devices present particular challenges.** Any mobile device with Internet connectivity is a potential problem. It is not good for a boy to be able to take a laptop or iPad or even a smart phone off by himself to view images. It is not fair to place this level of temptation in the hands of a boy or young man passing through puberty, making it possible for him to have any image on the Internet available to see in a matter of seconds.

- **Filters and parental controls.** Use filters and parental controls on the Internet.

- **Strong family culture.** It is desirable that there be a family culture of reading, with watching screens kept to a minimum. It can, however, be a great family activity to watch a good film together and then discuss it. Family members should not feel free to turn on the television or computer and start watching whatever seems interesting at the moment. Video viewing should be planned, social events.

- **Helping honest children to stay honest.** Even the best prudential steps to avoid problems in regard to human sexuality by governing one's home well can only help keep an honest child honest. If an individual intentionally seeks exposure to content of a certain sort, he will be able to get it, despite the best parental efforts. There is much more to educating and forming a son than simply helping him avoid inappropriate content. Indeed, focusing too much on this negative task can be deforming if it reinforces avoidance at the expense of the positive message that God's plan for human sexuality is good.

Teens and Dating

As their children become young adults, parents must carefully consider how they will handle dating. On the one hand, most would agree that parents who forbid their high school age sons and daughters all interaction with the opposite sex are being too strict and risk rebellion and other problems. On the other hand, intimate romances among high school age couples rarely end well.

By its very nature, an exclusive personal relationship between a man and a woman is ordered to marriage and can only be fulfilled completely through marriage and all it involves. Ideally, a young man and a young woman would only begin such a relationship with the intention of discerning a vocation to marriage. If marriage is impractical at the time and for the foreseeable future, any exclusive relationship has a built-in tension that is unfair to the couple. Although long courtships have sometimes led to stable and happy marriages, this is rare and can be difficult. For every high school couple that has ended up happily marrying after college, there are many more cases of broken hearts and sadness. Problems associated with high school romance can impact all areas of life: academic, social, family, ethical, and faith-related.

So how should parents navigate these challenging waters? What guidance should they provide their high school age children? No foolproof set of guidelines exists, but the following points can be helpful:

- **Plan group activities.** One healthy way for high school age young men and young women to interact is in groups engaged in doing something together that has real human value. Parents might open their homes to a planned event such as a game night with board games or charades. A group ice-skating or sledding excursion could work well. Youth groups in local churches often sponsor events with a high tone, including service activities. Such events can be great fun and a healthy way for teens to interact.

- **Parental rules about couple dating.** Some parents establish clear rules forbidding their children to date someone until a certain age or until given specific permission. Such a rule provides specific guidance by establishing that it is not acceptable for a high school student of a particular age to form an exclusive attachment by dating one particular person. The key downside of exercising parental authority via rules is the danger of an overly legalistic approach. A teenager, who longs for the day when, a senior now, he can ask a girl he likes to "go steady," can miss the crucial point that the gradual development of a dating relationship is a way of discerning the vocation to marriage. It is preferable that a high school student has a trusting relationship with his parents and asks them for advice and guidance regarding dating. Parents can still say no to something even if there is not a clear rule established ahead of time.

- **Practical expectations.** Parents should educate their children in good manners between men and women. Some norms that governed interactions between men and women in the past are now largely forgotten (for instance: when walking with a woman, a man should always place himself between the woman and the street), but others are still generally recognized (a man should hold a door for a woman). Parents must decide which traditional norms to convey to their children and which can be ignored. However, one norm that should be followed and emphasized above all others: unless they are brother and sister, at no time should a young man and a young woman ever be together alone in a private place behind a closed door.

- **Father-son and mother-daughter conversations on dating and vocation.** A father should have another planned talk with his son before his first date, which might be the school prom (see below). A mother should do the same with her daughter. This is best done while speaking again about vocation— following God's plan for one's life as the best way to happiness. Here is the most important thing parents can do to help their teenage sons and daughters in this area.

The Father-Son Conversation prior to the First Date

Parents who wish to avoid the extremes of forbidding all interaction between the sexes and allowing their children to enter into exclusive personal dating relationships will often find that the school prom, typically during the junior and senior year, provides the first dating situation. The prom ideally is a dignified event where dating couples are with their peers in a setting with a higher tone than a typical high school dance (these latter are not recommended). Some schools do things to foster this higher tone, such as beginning with a sit-down dinner and hiring a live band. In some cases, there are even dancing lessons. The prom can be an excellent way of training young people how to interact in a more formal setting.

Prior to the prom (or other occasion of a first date), a father-son conversation could cover the following points:

- **Start with vocation.** "It is a great joy for your mother and me to see you growing up a responsible young man who is seeking to discern God's will for his life; we are proud of you. Keep praying to know God's will. Your mother and I fully support whatever your vocation is; it is a great privilege for us to see God's plan for you unfolding. A call of total dedication to God through a celibate vocation is a higher calling—and a very beautiful one—and if God is calling you to this, great happiness (and suffering—as with any vocation) await if you accept the call. Marriage is also a wonderful vocation and a tremendous way by which God calls many to holiness. The vocation to marriage is particularly important in today's world, given the need for Christian families to spread the light of Christ into the very fabric of society (St. John Paul II went so far as to say, 'The family is the way for the Church.')."

- **Guarding the eyes and heart.** "One's eyes and heart must be guarded to keep the heart clean and whole for one's future vocation. If this vocation is marriage, one's heart should be kept 'locked with seven locks' until it can be truly given to that one special woman. On a date, guarding the heart means caring for the other person with refinement and good manners, in a chivalrous way. It also means avoiding anything that could lead to arousal, which may or may not happen because of physical contact. If arousal starts, the appropriate response is to avoid that type of contact in as natural a way as possible, even if the contact is only holding hands. It is seriously wrong to do anything on purpose that leads to sexual arousal; these motions of the body are meant for the marriage act, and initiating them outside marriage is an abuse of God's gift of sexuality."

- **Dating and discerning marriage.** "An exclusive and close relationship with a woman makes sense when discerning marriage. But be aware that such a relationship is naturally ordered to marriage and can only be fulfilled completely through marriage and all that this union involves. Ideally, a young man and a young woman would only begin such a relationship if the intention is to be open to discerning a vocation to marriage. If their circumstances make marriage impractical now and for the foreseeable future, any close relationship between them has a built-in tension that is unfair to the couple. In such situations, it is best to remain friends without becoming romantically involved. Although long courtships have sometimes led to stable and happy marriages, this is rare and can be difficult. For every high school couple who have ended up happily marrying after college, there are many more cases of broken hearts and sadness. Too many high school students who become involved in intimate relationships end up broken-hearted, depressed, or worse. All areas of life—academic, social, family, ethical, and faith-related—can be adversely affected."

- **Finding the right woman.** "If your vocation is to marry, it is important to choose your spouse wisely. Relying on romantic feelings alone is risky. Look not only for someone to whom you are attracted but who is your equal, with whom you can converse about important things. Look for someone who is virtuous and whom you believe would be a good mother to your children. Follow your heart to a certain extent, but do not forget to use your reason as well. Does this person share your outlook on reality, so that you will be able together to pass on a strong family culture to your children? Will this person help you grow closer to God? Do you and she agree on truly important things? Does she believe marriage is forever? Is she open to children?"

CHAPTER 7

THE FATHER AND HIS DAUGHTERS

A son obviously benefits from the attention of his father. He thrives when Dad makes time for him: playing catch, taking him on a hike, even involving him in repair jobs around the house. Some younger boys are very interested in watching their father using power tools and feel important when they can hand things to Dad. It is good for fathers to show affection for their sons physically, even wrestling with them when they are little. Lots of time together and close mentoring are important for a strong father-son relationship.

A strong relationship between a father and his daughter, though different, is also of critical importance. A father's mentoring of his sons involves lots of "doing;" his mentoring of his daughters involves primarily "being their father," although with some "doing" as well. Daughters look to their fathers to see the ideal of manhood, to see what it means to be a strong and responsible man in the world. For this reason, your influence on your daughter will depend a lot on who you are. If you are a strong man, with the heart of a father, your daughters will look up to you as their hero and protector. They will try to emulate your strength and values; one might even say your strength will make them strong. They will strive to please you and live up to your expectations for them. How you affirm them and what you compliment them for will contribute directly to how they see themselves and what they strive to accomplish.

An excellent book that makes this point and others is *Strong Fathers, Strong Daughters* by Dr. Meg Meeker. Dr. Meeker cites a wealth of studies showing the powerful positive influence that fathers have on their daughters. She also displays an excellent grasp of the dynamic that informs this critical relationship. As her title indicates, a strong and protective father who exercises authority is exactly what your daughter needs.

Here are some practical ways in which fathers can have a tremendous positive impact on their daughters' lives:

- **Showing affection.** To show affection for one's daughters is so natural that it typically just happens. Little girls are adorable, especially when they climb all over their daddy and soak up his embraces. If this type of physical affirmation does not come naturally to you, it is likely that your daughters will find a way to bring out this new side of your personality. If not, just pick them up and toss them gently over your head, catching them as they fall. The security a little girl feels in knowing that she is safe in the strong arms of her father powerfully communicates a positive view of human love and even of reality. My six-year-old daughter, Lucy, regularly comes up to me and holds her arms up with the smiling command, "Hold me, Daddy!" She loves to be picked up and carried.

- **Be careful about how you praise her.** Your daughter very much wants to hear spoken affirmation from you. Spoken words are very important to women, and your daughter is no exception. If you are a strong man of virtue, you probably have no idea how much she admires you and longs for your respect and compliments. And thus, you have no idea how important it is that you compliment her for the right things. Internalizing your spoken affirmations and forming her self-image from what you say, she will try to become more of what you compliment her for. So do not routinely praise her for something superficial, such as her physical beauty or her good grades. The father who tells his daughter he is pleased that she has lost weight runs the risk of leading her to focus in an unhealthy way on watching what she eats. The father who praises his daughter for her good grades will likely see his daughter trying harder to do well in school so as to further impress her father. This also can be unhealthy. Of course, it is a good idea once in a while to tell your teenage daughter that she is smart and beautiful. But the best praise you can give her concerns who she is as a person, how she cares for others, how she values the truth, how she is becoming a strong woman focused on what is right. If she thinks she needs to do something particular to impress you, she will try to do it and measure her self-worth against this standard. If you compliment her for who she is, for her strong character, you will be giving her permission to be a strong woman secure in who she is as one loved by her family and ultimately loved as a daughter of God. My high school age daughter Theresa, a responsible and hardworking student who does quite well, was becoming overly stressed about her schoolwork. I realized that I might be putting too much pressure on her, not directly but simply because as an educator I value academic excellence. I started talking to her about balance in one's life, about not getting too caught up in one's work and instead focusing more on the people around us. I complimented her on her kindness and service to our family and most of all on having her priorities right, with strong faith and rock solid loyalty to her friends. Without ceasing to put forth a very strong effort into her schoolwork, she stopped worrying about it so much. She worked hard but was detached from the results. I had helped her see that true learning is not just about doing well in school but in seeing reality correctly. We went back to talking about the problems with reductionism and how some of her classes, like chemistry, adopted an overly reductionistic perspective. The same strong Theresa was back, confident and truly seeking the good in her education.

- **Be strong in protecting her.** Like boys, girls typically go through a period of development in which they seek more independence and control. This is a normal part of growing up. Your daughter may insist on having more freedom to spend time with her friends, perhaps late in the evening. She may insist on being allowed to form friendships with young men her age or even to begin dating. While there is a legitimate side to a teenager's desire for independence, any father knows that she is vulnerable and needs parental wisdom and guidance. Left on her own, she could easily find herself in a situation where a young man could take advantage of her or she could be subject to some other danger. Speak with her about the clear and reasonable guidelines you and your wife insist she follow. She may not see them as reasonable, but it will help if you remind her that you have much more life experience than she does and are looking out for her from loving concern. She knows, at least deep down, that she is vulnerable and in need of protection. One way for her to express rebellion may be to test your love and protective care. "Does Dad really love me enough to stand up to my complaints, arguments, and the 'silent treatment' that I give him?" She needs you to be both reasonable and strong, even though she may not seem to want it. After reading this chapter, my fifteen-year-old daughter Theresa told me I should emphasize that if a father is strong in protecting his daughter, giving her clear guidelines in spite of her objections, their relationship may temporarily seem damaged but in the long run it will be strengthened. And the strengthening will likely come sooner rather than later. One of my colleagues at work recently told me how he and a friend "rescued" a young woman at a college party. She was from a strong family with solid values, which she shared, but unfortunately she drank too much at a party and found herself in a room behind a locked door with a young man with only one thing on his mind. My colleague and his friend broke down the door, fortunately in time to stop what was happening. Then they insisted that some female friends of the young woman take her away from the party and take care of her. Next day, though very ashamed, she thanked them for saving her from such a great mistake. If you are not certain your daughter is sensible enough to avoid such a situation—and the small steps that lead there can be all too easily taken—be very careful about what you allow her to do. You cannot count on having protectors, like my colleague and his friend, come to the rescue.

- **One-on-one time.** A father should take the time to treat his daughters as his little princesses, letting them know he greatly enjoys their presence and wants to hear about their joys and concerns. Every so often, a father should take each of his daughters out for some one-on-one time, a "date" of sorts. It need not be fancy: a simple Saturday morning trip to a local coffee shop or a short walk through a park. The important thing is that the father treats his daughter as a "little lady," with refinement and good manners. He should hold open the car door for her, ask her if she is comfortable, if the heat or air conditioning in the car should be adjusted or if she would rather have windows open, and inquire as to what kind of treat she would like most before purchasing it for her. He should ask her about how she is enjoying her studies and what interests her. No "agenda" is necessary; just spend time with her making polite small talk and giving her your undivided attention. Think of little details by which to be attentive to her preferences. This time with your daughter may not seem productive or formative, especially by comparison with personal mentoring fathers should give their sons. But nothing could be further from the truth. The simple goodness with which you treat your daughter will become the standard by which she judges any man who pays attention to her. When a young man takes her out on a date, she will judge him by how well he compares to you. You will be spreading a strong field of protection around her, causing her to expect to be treated with refinement and respect, and leading her to reject the attentions of any man who lacks this refinement and genuine concern for her wellbeing. And all this is so easy to do! There is hardly more to it than treating her as your little princess and giving her individual attention once in a while.

- **Take an interest in her education.** Some fathers scrutinize the academic achievements of their sons but downplay the importance of the education of their daughters. Fathers know their sons may well have to support families with their professional work, and sound academic preparation is important for that. But it is a mistake for a father to attach little importance to the education of his daughters. She may become a doctor, a lawyer, a businesswoman, a teacher, or a professional in some other field requiring a high level of education. Even if she marries and puts her profession on hold or works part-time while caring for her young children, she will likely spend a significant amount of time during her life doing professional work outside the home. More importantly, education is not just preparation for professional work. It is about learning what is true for its own sake, and education enriches one's humanity. This is particularly so today, when reductive patterns of thought overemphasize the utility of knowledge. A well-educated woman with a trained intellect is better able to live as a woman of faith and culture, better equipped to care for others and be a true steward of humanity.

- **Reinforce Mom's authority.** Just as you will spend lots of time closely mentoring your sons, your wife will naturally spend lots of time with your daughters. It is not uncommon for daughters and mothers to disagree and argue. This is normal. For the most part, you are well advised to stay out of their conversations and let them work matters out. If you are too quick to step in and support your wife, you risk alienating your daughter, especially if you do not acknowledge the legitimate points she makes. There are times, however, when your wife will need your help. As the father, you have a moral authority for some matters that your wife simply does not have. For example, if your daughter is fond of a particular outfit that is less than modest, she will be much more likely to listen to your reasons for her not to wear that outfit than to her mother's. Tell her you are not comfortable with how men will look at her dressed that way. Coming from you, this message will have authority and be taken seriously. If there is a strong disagreement between your daughter and your wife on something, and you see that you need to back up your wife, it is best if you talk privately with your daughter. Reason with her. Explain the situation from her mom's perspective. This is generally a much better approach than making an authoritative public pronouncement in favor of your wife's position.

- **Meet her date.** When she is old enough to date, you should insist on meeting the young man as soon as possible. If she is still living under your roof, it is reasonable that you require that he come in and meet you. Look the fellow in the eye. Give him a firm handshake. Engage him in small talk. And before they leave, make sure you have asked him what his plans for the evening are and when your daughter will get home. When they return, be there ready to talk to him again, looking him in the eye. You can get a sense of his character from how he handles himself when talking to you. He will get the message that your daughter is precious in your eyes and you intend to protect her. Even if you like the young man very much, it is important to keep up this friendly practice of formally asking about plans for the evening and then meeting him afterwards.

A father who treats his daughter this way will gain her respect; she will look to him as her hero protector and form her worldview with him in mind. She will be very interested in his opinions. He will have a great deal of moral authority with her. If a father is strongly committed to what is true and right, his daughter will strive to emulate his virtues. An occasional word from him on what is right or wrong will be all that is needed for her to internalize a right outlook on reality. Even if she goes through a bit of a rough time—perhaps even some teenage rebellion—a father's attention and guidance will make a decisive difference. She may roll her eyes at her mother's suggestions, but as long as she knows her father looks on her with tender love, she will never stray very far.

Without affection and affirmation from her father, however, she will typically seek them from another man, often in an unhealthy way. If she receives affirmation from her father, she will naturally be led toward someone like him, who will love her for who she is and respect her as a person. The love of God the Father will also find a welcome place in her heart as she grows into a woman of faith.

CHAPTER 8

THE FATHER IN SUPPORT OF HIS CHILDREN'S VOCATIONS

All earthly fatherhood is a participation in the complete fatherhood present in the inner life of the Trinity. From this reality two distinct, perhaps even seemingly contradictory, things follow. First, since God's fatherhood is fatherhood in the true and perfect sense, the fatherhood of an earthly father is necessarily limited and imperfect. Those who argue that the experience of human fatherhood provides a culturally conditioned metaphor for understanding God (so that speaking of God's fatherhood communicates little or nothing to those who lack a good experience of human fatherhood) have it completely backwards: it is God's fatherhood that is perfect and the reference point for us to understand imperfect human fatherhood. Secondly, since the very nature of earthly fatherhood is rooted in a more perfect divine fatherhood, it participates in the greatest of realities and is ennobled beyond what we can comprehend in this life.

It takes humility for a father to accept that his earthly fatherhood is limited and imperfect. In each father's heart, itself wounded by sin, there is a tendency to want to claim for itself rights and status, especially regarding his children as they enter adulthood, that are not fully his. It is easy for a father to forget that he is merely passing through this life on a journey. Many fathers form plans for their children's future. Some of these plans are reasonable and good, and often fathers are able to give older children good fatherly advice, professional and otherwise, as they begin to set out on their paths in the world. But it is easy to go too far, to try to control a child's future, to try to pressure him or her to follow a particular path.

Fathers do not have the right or the authority to interfere with a child's freedom to follow his or her vocation, which is a great gift from God. A father is called to love his children, to care for them when they are young, to pray for them always, to talk and listen to them, to encourage them, and to let them know that the most important thing in organizing their lives is that they follow the path God has chosen, their vocation. As Mary could embrace her vocation, giving her "fiat," when she was a young teenager, so teenage children who have been well formed can see and choose the path God has chosen for them. A good father should tell his children openly that the most important thing in their lives is to follow God's will in this matter of vocation. And he will say this with a great deal of confidence and optimism, emphasizing that those who generously follow God are rewarded with great joy. Some suffering too, of course, but the suffering becomes the Holy Cross for those who are close to God, and he bears most of its weight.

An earthly father exercises his imperfect fatherhood by entrusting his child to the perfect, providential fatherhood of God. He is like the steward who has governed a kingdom for a time but is now passing his charge on to the newly crowned king. This can be difficult, especially for hearts wounded by sin, for fathers who want to continue to govern and protect their children.

But here human fatherhood is lived to the fullest. A good father wants what is best for his children. He wants them to be well cared for, with enough of the material necessities, to grow in virtue and responsibility, and to find their path in the world. No father, however, is really able to provide all these things on his own. As he begins to age, he will notice signs of his mortality. He will know that prosperity is easily lost, that the future is uncertain, and there is no guarantee that he will be able to provide well for his family for the next several years, much less provide for his children until they are grown.

All this is an invitation to prepare his children for life as best he can, then turn them over to God's loving care. Abraham's sacrifice of his son Isaac (see Gen 22:1–19), to what he thought was God's will, provides an example here. Moreover, a father's hopes for his child may be significantly different from the path his child discerns. This can happen in professional matters (a father hopes his son will become an engineer but his son pursues studio art). Or it can happen when a father hopes his daughter will marry and she discerns a single vocation as her path. In such cases the father is asked to sacrifice his own desires, giving control over to God.

This surrender, especially if embraced with love, is the highest expression of fatherhood in that it most directly participates in the fatherhood of God. Part of God's fatherly care is to respect our freedom. He who is all powerful, all good, and all loving, allows his creatures to choose freely. He clearly sees the suffering sin causes, yet he patiently has prepared a way for suffering to be swallowed up in victory without removing the freedom whose abuse has caused the suffering. A human father who gives his children willingly up to God's plan is modeling the way God also respects and supports the great gift of freedom.

The following are some important messages a father should communicate to his older children, thus opening the way for them lovingly to embrace their vocations:

- **Express your love and your confidence that it is good for your son or daughter to enter adulthood.** "Your mother and I are proud of you and love you. When you were small you needed our help for the simplest things. Now you are entering adulthood. It is a great joy for us to see you becoming a fine young man (or woman). You are getting ready to set out in the world on your own. If your mother cries a bit when you leave for college, do not be surprised. The tears are mostly happy ones, although there will certainly be times when we miss you a lot."

- **Express your faith in God's providence.** "We know that God has a plan for you and your life. It is an awesome thing for a parent to see his child growing up a man (or woman) of God. We have seen signs of strong faith at work in your life (mention some). Though we do not know what God's plan for you is, we do know that the most important thing is that you follow the path God has chosen for you. We will continue to pray that you discover God's plan for you."

- **Challenge your child actively to seek his or her vocation.** "You also need to pray to know your vocation and for the grace to follow it with a generous heart. Do so every day. God does not usually announce their vocations to people directly and all at once. St. Paul was an exception, and he was already a zealous man of God. Typically, though, God draws the heart by much more gentle means, opening a possibility that can be followed or not and showing a tremendous respect for freedom. He shows the prayerful heart that perhaps he or she can serve him and others in such and such a way. If the person starts to follow this path, more light and peace come. Soon, and by small steps, a vocational calling grows in the soul. This is how you will likely see the path that God has in mind for you. And you will be free to follow it in love or not. If you choose another path, God will not abandon you, but you will not be as happy and others will miss out on the gift that your vocation could have been for them."

- **Marriage.** "Marriage is a beautiful vocation, yet some enter into marriage by default, not really trying to discern God's will for their lives. Still, God blesses human love and wants to raise it to the level of a great sacrament; he will do this for a couple if they let him, even if they did not come together in response to discerning his will. It is better, however, to receive this vocation as a positive call. This can be a wonderful beginning to a happy marriage. Today there is a great need for holy marriages to witness to the world the integrity of human love. St. John Paul II emphasized this by saying the family is the way for the Church today."

- **Single vocations.** "God calls some select souls to single vocations, which are higher callings than vocations to marriage. Many such vocations are oriented to serve and strengthen marriages as well. The Church, which is the Body of Christ, grows through each member living out his or her particular calling. If you are called to forgo marriage for the sake of the Kingdom of God—and so are called to celibacy—you will be very much on the front lines of the battles the Church is fighting in our time. God will be with you, supporting you in whatever tasks he has for you to accomplish. Your mother and I will be greatly honored if God has chosen one of our children for such a great and holy work. You can always count on our support and especially our prayers."

- **True joy and the cross.** "All vocations involve great joy and some suffering. God is not outdone in generosity. He will reward those who abandon everything to follow the path he has chosen for their lives. As the Gospel says, those who embark on this great adventure receive great rewards both in this life and in the life to come. Every vocational path involves some suffering. But for those children of God who are close to him, even suffering comes with joy. It is a great joy to be close to him, even when helping him carry the cross. The suffering of the children of God is much different from the suffering of those who live without God. These latter may find some limited happiness for a time, but when suffering comes, as it inevitably will, it will be difficult for them to see any meaning in it, and it can be isolating and even lead to despair. The mystery of suffering is an invitation to persons of good will to seek a deeper meaning in life. Those of us who are fortunate enough to live as children of God should offer friendship and direction to such souls."

CHAPTER 9

PREPARING ONE'S HEART FOR MATURE FATHERHOOD IN MARRIAGE

The most important marriage preparation a young man can engage in is the interior work of preparing his heart. The human heart longs to be attached to what it perceives as good. The challenge is that what we perceive as the desired good is often a limited good or even something that could be harmful. Yet the heart is made for love and to love rightly. Preparation of one's heart thus has two distinct dimensions: guarding it so as to save it for the other, and educating it so that it embraces what is truly good in the right way. Guarding keeps the heart from making attachments that are distractions from a greater good or, much worse, adhering to something that debases the heart, while education enables one's heart to grow into a father's heart.

Guarding the Heart

The first step in guarding a heart is to recognize what that means and why it is necessary. Guarding one's heart fundamentally consists in the continual performance of interior acts of refusing to allow it to form an attachment to what it perceives as desirable when one's reason knows that should not be done. These interior acts are supported by prudential exterior actions as well, such as not placing oneself in a situation where the heart will be overly tempted by what it inordinately desires. For example, it makes sense for a married man to avoid overly familiar conversations with attractive women at work, lest by small degrees his heart starts to form an attachment to someone other than his wife. The interior act of only allowing his heart to be for his wife is supported by confining his interactions with attractive female colleagues to professional matters.

Guarding one's heart is necessary because of the nature of the human heart in our present condition. We are always seeking happiness: there is a longing for some perceived good in even the most twisted desire of a human heart wounded by sin. We need to be savvy enough to know that happiness is not ultimately the result of getting whatever we want. This is obvious in the case of young children. A toddler may passionately want to have a particular toy or engage in some activity; when his desires are thwarted he becomes upset and perhaps even cries. But if he gets what he so badly wants, it only makes him happy for a short time before his wants shift to something else. In moving from one thing to another, he eventually becomes upset for no apparent reason, crying until someone picks him up and carries him away.

Something similar happens with young men and indeed with all people. A young man may think that a particular possession, such as a car or house, or a particular job, or even the companionship of a particular woman is essential to his happiness in life. And getting whatever it is may satisfy his heart for a longer time than a toy or a game satisfies a toddler. He may even think he has found happiness of a sort if all goes well for him and he is able to move ahead from success to success in realizing his life plan. If there is not deeper order and purpose to his life, however, at some point he will realize that his happiness is like a house built on a foundation of sand, easily swept away by the inevitable rough waves.

It is crucial to grasp that nothing in this world can ultimately satisfy one's heart, since the human heart is made for nothing less than friendship with God himself. St. Augustine said, addressing God: "You have made us for yourself and our hearts are restless until they rest in you."[8] Anything short of God is bound to

---

8. St. Augustine, *Confessions*, Book 1.

disappoint. So guarding one's heart involves a fundamental decision not to look to anything of this world for perfect satisfaction, to live with a knowing awareness that our hearts can ultimately find rest only in God.

This fundamental orientation of one's heart toward God is not the same as living in a constant state of stoic denial of all human loves. God is a loving and provident Father who wants his children to rejoice in the goodness of the created world, which he has given us as a gift. The Christian attitude toward the things of this world is that they are fundamentally good, that by analogy they reflect God's goodness, and that we are called to recognize, appreciate, and even to love created realities, but in a way consistent with what they are: gifts from the One who loves us. As such, they rightly call forth the appreciation of the human heart, but they are misused when the heart tries to take ownership of them on its own terms, failing to see their giftedness. Whatever in this world we want, whatever we think will make us happy, is limited in its ability to do so. It may be a very good thing, even something God intends for us to possess for a time and use, but it is not a final resting place for the heart.

On a practical level, the interior act of guarding one's heart from seeking rest and fulfillment in things of this world requires that one embark on a path that involves real self-denial. For us with hearts wounded by sin, guarding the heart requires following an ascetical plan where we habitually deny our wants, offering small acts of self-denial out of love for God and others. It means not overindulging in food or entertainment and at times fasting from certain foods (or eating more of what is less tasty) or from television or the computer. It also means setting aside time daily for prayer and being close to the sacraments of the Church. In short, it involves living a life "in Christ," as the guarding of one's heart is not something that we can do by our own power but only with the help of his grace.

It may seem contradictory that we need both to live a radical detachment and at the same time properly love the things of this world. In reality, the contradiction is only apparent. It is resolved when we realize that denying the heart attachments to lesser goods increases its freedom to love more noble things and ultimately to love God above all else and everything in its proper order for his sake. Far from being only a path of self-denial, the path of mortification to free the heart from attachments is also a path of great joy. St. Francis of Assisi was able to rejoice in the goodness of creation precisely because he was such a great ascetic. His detachment from the goods of this world and his life of penance and mortification made it possible for him to love all the creatures around him with youthful joy. He saw in all God's creation a goodness and beauty that could only be seen by a free heart not set on claiming possession and control. For us who live in the world, the act of claiming ownership, of setting one's heart on something as under one's control or dominion, while legitimate at times and to some extent, is harmful if the act of claiming the thing for one's self is done in such a way as to limit what it is to what it is for me.

Due to certain philosophical errors that have informed the way people today apprehend reality, loving things and persons properly is perhaps more difficult in our time than it was in previous centuries. To have a heart free for love, one that is not tied to something in an inordinate way, a person must fundamentally see and appreciate the thing or person loved as it is in itself, as a thing with a particular nature and its own perfections. Once the unique subjectivity of the other is appreciated, its limited possession in the right way becomes possible. Those who see the goodness of the thing in itself recognize that their ownership is merely temporary and that all the goods of this earth are ultimately to be used properly, taken care of, and passed on to future generations, or, in the case of other persons, loved in a way that always respects their unique dignity and freedom as children of God and thus never simply uses them.[9]

---

9. For more on the necessity of always respecting persons by continuing to recognize their unique dignity as human subjects who can never licitly be considered as mere objects, see Karol Wojtyla's *Love and Responsibility*.

Since early modern times, especially as a result of the work of Francis Bacon and Rene Descartes, a tendency to see things in simply mechanistic and functional terms has grown. A result of this way of apprehending reality is that things, and even persons, are often reduced from what they are in themselves, with their own particular natures and perfections, to what they are *for me.* To know a thing today it is less important to know what it is, what its nature is (formal causality), and how it is directed from within toward the rest of reality (final causality). Today, rather, the emphasis is on knowing how a thing functions and how its parts are mechanically arranged.

Thus intrinsic to the worldview of our time is a shift of attention from what the other is in itself and how it reflects in some way the goodness and beauty of its Creator, to how its functions can be known so as to be controlled. Such empirical knowledge of things is good and the technology to which it has given rise is likewise good, but there is need to integrate this knowledge into human knowledge more broadly considered. Limiting one's perspective on what is objective to what is known by the methods of the empirical sciences, as if these methods are the only valid means to reach truth, is an unwarranted reduction of human reason and of the human person.[10]

So when Bacon and Descartes set aside formal and final causality with the goal of developing useful knowledge, they set in motion a reductive way of knowing that makes it more difficult for the human heart to relate properly to reality, to reflect a Christian orientation toward the other that begins with respecting what the other is rather than making its meaning for me the most fundamental thing. The radical living of Christian detachment and the ascetical plan that supports it has always been important, but it is arguably more important now than it has ever been.

---

10. This is the main point that Pope Benedict makes in his frequently misunderstood "Regensburg Address."

Self-denial and detachment force the heart to give up its desire for inordinate ownership, of seeing the other as primarily "for me." This creates the necessary space for one to, first, recognize the goodness of the other as other before reducing it to its value for me. Self-denial, prayer, the sacraments (especially penance and the Eucharist), and, in short, a serious seeking of holiness are essential if one is to avoid reducing what something is in its givenness and relatedness to merely what it is for me. This is especially so for persons, for whom relation constitutes an arguably essential aspect of their being.

Guarding the Heart as a Preparation for Marriage

An important dimension of guarding one's heart as a preparation for marriage is becoming open to the possibility of receiving the vocation to marriage from God. God calls many young men to marriage, but many men pursue the path of marriage as simply following their natural affections and inclinations rather than as a path to be embraced as a calling from God.

It is not a bad thing for a young man to fall in love with a woman. God certainly wants to bless human love, and he will bless the human love of couples who are open to his becoming a part of their lives. Such couples will find a great divine purification of their human love, a gift by which it is raised to a higher level. The Church welcomes couples and invites them to move forward on their journey to discover a deeper dimension that God wants to give to their relationship.

But even though it is good for a man and woman to fall in love and then seek to make God a part of their relationship, it is even better for them to receive each other as a gift from God right from the start, to grow close together as a response to God's vocational calling. This is only possible for those who live a radical detachment of the heart from any particular life path. Only a young man willing to guard his heart from forming a premature attachment to a woman or even an attachment to the idea of marriage can truly receive marriage as a calling from God from the start of the relationship.

A young man should approach the question of his vocation with a heart not prematurely set on one single path, a heart detached from seeking comfort in any particular relationship before the right time. Such a heart has the freedom to embrace a vocation out of love. The heart best able to embrace a vocation, such as a vocation to marriage, is one that has been prepared by refusing to seek a resting place in anything less than God and his will. The man who is completely open to receiving his vocational calling from God, eager to follow his will for marriage or even a higher call, is the man who will be best able to respond, as Joseph did, to the call to "not be afraid to take this woman for your wife" (Mt 1:20).

Growing the Heart

In addition to the protective guarding of the heart, a young man needs to prepare for his vocation by educating his heart so that it becomes the heart of a father, a heart open to love. A father's heart is one that seeks to support, serve, and protect others out of one's own strength, and to exercise leadership through service to others. A father needs to work with dedication and purpose. He needs to be industrious, not lazy: a hard worker who sees a deeper meaning in his work done well. The fort building and play acting of boyhood should grow into the hardworking professionalism of a man striving to order his environment for the good of himself and others.

The moral imagination of a young man needs to expand to see his work in the light of professional service, service to his family or future family, his community, his country, the world at large, and to God. The pioneer adventure stories of youth should continue to resonate with him, tales of young men heading out into frontier lands and building a homestead, much as he is now heading out on his own professional path in the world.

A young man needs to continue to expand his moral imagination through reading well-chosen books. To be able to communicate a more human and upright path to others he will need to steep himself in excellent literature, philosophy, history, and books that present religious truths. If it is true in some sense that a person is what he eats, it is likewise true that the heart of a man is formed by what he reads, views, and hears. In a very fundamental sense it is what comes out of the heart, the actions one chooses, which defile or perfect the person.[11] Even so, these acts are formed in part by what a person takes into his heart by reading, inasmuch as reading helps to form his worldview. If a young man's professional work is technical in nature, it will be all the more important for him to continue to steep himself in the best of the humanities so as to grow as a person in a balanced way.

Of particular note is J. R. R. Tolkien's monumental work *The Lord of the Rings*. Tolkien wrote it with a father's heart, considering especially the need to properly educate his children. His trilogy was written as a way to counter the deficient and reductive aspects of the modern worldview and to help his children internalize a more complete and noble outlook on reality. Tolkien described it as an antidote to modernity. While not an allegory (Tolkien insisted on this point) the *Lord of the Rings* presents the struggle between good and evil as bracingly real yet carried on in the context of an overall providential purpose, a meaning discovered by the characters as they act out their proper roles. The decisions they make, far from being based on reductive and incomplete reasoning, take place against a horizon open to transcendence and the full scope of reality, a reality marred by the powerful forces of evil yet still fundamentally good and under a deeper providential purpose. The decision to carry the ring of power into the heart of the land of Mordor, to the very seat of the enemy's power, makes no sense unless there

---

11. "For out of the heart come evil thoughts, murder, adultery, fornication, theft, false witness, slander" (Mt 15:19).

is meaning to reality and a providential purpose that persons are to discover and live out. The work is characterized by a profound recognition of hierarchy in creation, a deep fundamental order to reality, the importance of upright moral action, being open to the full scope of what is true, noble, and beautiful, and even the importance of little things and little ones who apparently lack power but whose contribution to history can be decisive. In all these ways it is an invitation to rediscover the best aspects of how people viewed reality in a former time, which still resonates deeply with the hearts of men of our time.

Another book that I want particularly to recommend is Evelyn Waugh's classic *Brideshead Revisited*. Though very different from *Lord of the Rings*, Waugh's novel is also about the education of the human heart to perceive reality correctly. Waugh recognizes that a critical problem with modernity is the reductive outlook that renders a person incapable of apprehending that which is true, good, or beautiful. With a mix of humor and sharp wit, Waugh shows this depravity in the character of Rex, a savvy businessman who falls in love with Julia, a young woman from an old English Catholic family. Rex, having once seen a high Catholic wedding, decides that he wants to become Catholic so that he too can have the pomp of a rich liturgical marriage ceremony, complete "with guys wearing red." He begins taking catechism lessons from an elderly priest who quickly becomes baffled at how to reach his pupil. Rex is a very agreeable student; indeed, he seems to be ready to accept whatever the kindly priest says. But he is not capable of understanding what it means to believe something is true. In an attempt to get Rex to realize that truth claims have importance, the priest asks Rex what it would mean if the pope said it was raining but outside it was sunny. In that case, Rex answers, it must be raining spiritually. He expresses surprise that the priest seems bothered by his overly agreeable acceptance of Catholic doctrines and tells the priest that he does not know why he is being given a hard time since he is someone who can "do things" for Catholics.

Julia's younger sister, although still a child, picks up on Rex's peculiar deficiencies and playfully tries to make fun of the situation. She tells him that once he becomes Catholic he will always have to sleep with his feet facing east so that he can walk to heaven if he dies. He will also have to believe in sacred monkeys in the Vatican. Later in the story, after Rex and Julia break up, Julia says of Rex, "He wasn't a complete human being at all. He was a tiny bit of one, unnaturally developed; something in a bottle, an organ kept alive in a laboratory. I thought he was a sort of primitive savage, but he was something absolutely modern and up-to-date that only this ghastly age could produce. A tiny bit of a man pretending he was the whole."[12] As Waugh's type of the successful modern businessman, Rex shows himself incapable of understanding what truth is. He is horrifyingly practical and virtually devoid of any transcendence, a man nearly incapable of seeing and appreciating what is, a reductive shell of a man who is the logical product of the philosophy of Bacon and Descartes.

Brideshead Revisited has more to offer, however, than a horrifying vision of reductive man and a description of the "Hooper style" education that helps form him. Waugh does not portray the true, good, noble, and beautiful in the same manner as Tolkien, but the reader who understands that the real hero of the story is Divine Providence can see glimpses of nobility in the broken lives of characters who can be called back to the truth by "the twitch of a thread."

Feeding the heart with reading that prepares it to see and love reality rightly is important, but forming the heart to love rightly is fundamentally the work of growing in holiness, a work God does in us. A young man needs to turn to God in prayer, receive the sacraments, and serve others through the corporal and spiritual works of mercy. All this educates and expands the heart, preparing it for marriage or any other vocation.

---

12. Evelyn Waugh, *Brideshead Revisited* (New York: Little, Brown and Company, 1973), 200.

Conclusion

Fatherhood is a natural reality that, through one's vocation, is taken up into the supernatural order of grace. A man experiences fatherhood on the natural level as something built into his nature as a male person. It is expressed in the desire of each man to exercise dominion through service and to form others to participate in this mission. God calls each man, giving him a specific vocation to live his fatherhood in a particular way, as a father of a family, a priest, or in some other way. His friendship with God—the essence of holiness—is in some way rooted in living as a father, thus participating in the perfect fatherhood of God.

This book has primarily focused on the vocation to fatherhood lived in a family, as husband of a wife and father of children. Living up to the demands of family life is challenging for a father. It can be hard for a tired man to continue to give of himself after a long day at work, especially when he just wants to relax, sit in front of a screen, newspaper, or book, and tune the world out. But the consequences of neglecting the duties of father and husband are all too apparent. There would be much less suffering in families today if fathers truly lived their fatherhood. And with God's grace, a father can find great joy in generously giving of himself to the others.

In attempting to define and describe fatherhood and explain how it should be lived, it is easy to strongly imply that a particular trait is intrinsic to manhood when it is also connected to authentic femininity. If I have done this, I apologize. I mean no slight to the dignity of women, motherhood, or the real strength of women. Understanding true fatherhood sheds light on the beauty of a woman's vocation to motherhood, and the complementarity of the two.

But it is important to speak about the essentials of fatherhood and motherhood. Discussion of empirical studies has its place, but we must employ the full scope of language and reason to talk about the realities behind the data. For perhaps the first time in history, we are in danger of no longer being able to apprehend the natural world, with its own order and rich meaning for human relationships. When reason is reduced to recognizing only the methods of the empirical sciences as valid for reaching truth, we are at risk of becoming insensitive to deeper human meaning and end up understanding reality primarily in functional terms.

I am aware that there are those who believe the best way to argue for a traditional view of marriage is to primarily employ the methods of the empirical sciences. They note that some current sociological data shows that living traditional family values results in demonstrable benefits across a broad spectrum of metrics. And while this is true now and even points toward the deeper meaning of such realities as fatherhood and motherhood, if we see fatherhood and motherhood only in functional terms, we stand on very shaky ground for the future.

But, rooted in the creative wisdom of God, the meaning of fatherhood and the rest of the natural order cannot change. No matter how far efforts proceed to define existence on new principles, language reflecting openness to the fullness of reality, to the natural world and order, will always have the potential of resonating in the human heart. In other words, metaphysics, understood as the science of being and employing the full scope of reason to seek to understand reality—with an openness to natural forms and finality—should not be set aside in speaking of profound human realities. Fighting the radical program of those who seek to redefine humanity only with data and statistics that show the superiority of traditional ways is like fighting a raging forest fire by burning the fuel in its path as a containment strategy. It may be a part of an overall strategy; but what is really needed is the cool mountain waters to flood the land, extinguishing the fires, and nourishing the soil for new growth. What is needed is the use of language that moves beyond mechanisms and overreliance on efficient causality to a deeper understanding of reality, an understanding that is metaphysical and open to the fullness of being, including the formal and final causality, which has been unnecessarily set aside in modern thought.

The present attempt to describe the nature of fatherhood falls far short of a flood of life-giving water. It may only be a small brook that disappears into the raging flames. My hope is that it will encourage others with much more talent to add their voices—fully rational ones—to the conversation. In times past, when the issue was the meaning of the natural order, a reductive modern form of reasoning may have been enough to convince. Today, the question is becoming whether nature understood as a stable objective reality even exists. Yet even now some people recognize the order of nature on a deep level. It is no accident that Pope Francis, in his encyclical *Laudato Si*, has invited those with profound respect for the natural environment to value nature consistently in areas of human ecology as well. With the full consistency of integral human reason, a reason open to the fullness of being, we can again speak a language that resonates in the hearts of men and women of goodwill in our times.

Appendix

Resources for a Father Teaching His Children

Michael's list of top books to read out loud with the family:

Literature

1. J. R. R Tolkien, *The Lord of the Rings* (trilogy)
2. Ralph Moody, *Little Britches* and the books which follow in the series
3. C. S. Lewis, *The Chronicles of Narnia*
4. Ernestine Gilbreth Carey and Frank Bunker Gilbreth Jr., *Cheaper by the Dozen*
5. C. S. Lewis, *Out of the Silent Planet* and *Perelandra* (the third book in the series That Hideous Strength is a fine book but does not work as well as a family read aloud book)
6. Jane Austen, *Pride and Prejudice*
7. Laura Ingalls Wilder, *Farmer Boy* and other books
8. Roald Dahl, *Matilda*
9. Jim Kjelgaard, *Big Red* and other books
10. Baroness Orczy, *The Scarlet Pimpernel*
11. Kenneth Grahame, *The Wind in the Willows*
12. William O. Steele, *Winter Danger* and other books

Lives of the Saints

1. William Thomas Walsh, *Our Lady of Fatima*
2. John Coverdale, *Uncommon Faith: The Early Years of Opus Dei* (1928–1943)
3. Ignatius Press, *Vision Books* Series
4. Louis de Wohl, *The Quiet Light* and some of his other books
5. Tan Books' *Lives of the Saints for Children* series

Michael's list of things to memorize with children:

The Ten Commandments

1. I am the Lord your God: You shall not have strange gods before me.
2. You shall not take the name of the Lord your God in vain.
3. Remember to keep holy the Lord's Day.
4. Honor your father and your mother.
5. You shall not kill.
6. You shall not commit adultery.
7. You shall not steal.
8. You shall not bear false witness against your neighbor.
9. You shall not covet your neighbor's wife.
10. You shall not covet your neighbor's goods.

The seven sacraments

1. Baptism
2. Confirmation
3. Holy Eucharist
4. Reconciliation
5. Anointing of the Sick
6. Holy Orders
7. Marriage

The definition of a sacrament

A sacrament is an outward sign instituted by Christ to give grace.

The seven Corporal Works of Mercy

1. Feeding the hungry
2. Giving drink to the thirsty
3. Clothing the naked
4. Sheltering the homeless
5. Visiting the sick
6. Visiting the imprisoned
7. Burying the dead

The seven Spiritual Works of Mercy

1. Counseling the doubtful
2. Instructing the ignorant
3. Admonishing sinners
4. Comforting the afflicted
5. Forgiving offenses
6. Bearing wrongs patiently
7. Praying for the living and the dead

The four Cardinal Virtues

1. Prudence
2. Temperance
3. Fortitude
4. Justice

The three Theological Virtues

1. Faith
2. Hope
3. Charity

The Beatitudes

1. Blessed are the poor in spirit, for theirs is the kingdom of heaven.
2. Blessed are those who mourn, for they shall be comforted.
3. Blessed are the meek, for they shall inherit the earth.
4. Blessed are those who hunger and thirst for righteousness, for they shall be satisfied.
5. Blessed are the merciful, for they shall obtain mercy.
6. Blessed are the pure in heart, for they shall see God.
7. Blessed are the peacemakers, for they shall be called sons of God.
8. Blessed are those who are persecuted for righteousness' sake, for theirs is the kingdom of heaven.
9. Blessed are you when men revile you and persecute you and utter all kinds of evil against you falsely on my account. Rejoice and be glad, for your reward is great in heaven.

A question from the Baltimore Catechism, "Why did God make me?"

God made me to know Him, to love Him, and to serve Him in this world and to be happy with Him forever in the next.

Three miracles that take place at every Mass

1. The changing of the substance of the bread and wine to the substance of Jesus Christ.
2. The withholding of the accidents of Jesus Christ. (The Eucharist is the only substance that does not typically display its own accidents.)
3. The preservation of the accidents of the bread and wine so that our senses continue to perceive mere bread and wine.

Basic vocal prayers:

Our Father

Our Father, who art in heaven, hallowed be thy name. Thy kingdom come; thy will be done on earth as it is in heaven. Give us this day our daily bread; and forgive us our trespasses as we forgive those who trespass against us; and lead us not into temptation, but deliver us from evil. Amen.

Hail Mary

Hail, Mary, full of grace, the Lord is with thee; blessed art thou among women, and blessed is the fruit of thy womb, Jesus. Holy Mary, Mother of God, pray for us sinners, now and at the hour of our death. Amen.

Glory Be

Glory be to the Father, and to the Son, and to the Holy Spirit. As it was in the beginning, is now, and ever shall be, world without end. Amen.

Angel of God

Angel of God, my guardian dear, to whom God's love commits me here, ever this day be at my side, to light and guard, to rule and guide. Amen.

Memorare

Remember, O most gracious Virgin Mary, that never was it known that anyone who fled to thy protection, implored thy help, or sought thy intercession was left unaided. Inspired by this confidence, I fly unto thee, O Virgin of virgins, my Mother. To thee I come, before thee I stand, sinful and sorrowful. O Mother of the Word incarnate, despise not my petitions, but in thy mercy hear and answer me. Amen.

Salve Regina

Hail, holy Queen, mother of mercy, our life, our sweetness, and our hope. To thee do we cry, poor, banished children of Eve. To thee do we send up our sighs, mourning and weeping in this valley of tears. Turn then, O most gracious advocate, thine eyes of mercy toward us, and after this our exile show unto us the blessed fruit of thy womb, Jesus. O clement, O loving, O sweet Virgin Mary, pray for us, O most holy Mother of God, that we may be made worthy of the promises of Christ. Amen.

Michael's family